PRAISE FOR MIKE SAGER

"Sager plays Virgil in the modern American Inferno . . . Compelling and stylish magazine journalism, rich in novelistic detail."

—*Kirkus Reviews*

"Like his journalistic precursors Tom Wolfe and Hunter S. Thompson, Sager writes frenetic, off-kilter pop-sociological profiles of Americans in all their vulgarity and vitality . . . He writes with flair, but only in the service of an omnivorous curiosity and defies expectations in pieces that lesser writers would play for satire or sensationalism . . . A Whitmanesque ode to teeming humanity's mystical unity."

—*The New York Times Book Review*

"I once described Mike Sager as 'the Beat poet of American journalism.' The title is still apt. For decades, he has explored the beautiful and horrifying underbelly of American society with poignantly explicit portrayals of porn stars, swingers, druggies, movie stars, rockers, and rappers, as well as stunning stories about obscure people whose lives were resonant with deep meaning—a 92-year-old man, an extraordinarily beautiful woman, a 650-pound man. He became a journalistic ethnographer of American life and his generation's heir to the work of Gay Talese, Tom Wolfe, and Hunter S. Thompson. His imposing body of work today is collected in more than a dozen books and eBooks."

—Walt Harrington, author and past head of Journalism at the University of Illinois

ALSO BY MIKE SAGER

NONFICTION

Scary Monsters and Super Freaks: Stories of Sex, Drugs, Rock 'n' Roll, and Murder

Revenge of the Donut Boys: True Stories of Lust, Fame, Survival, and Multiple Personality

The Someone You're Not: True Stories of Sports, Celebrity, Politics & Pornography

Stoned Again: The High Times and Strange Life of a Drugs Correspondent

Vetville: True Stories of the U.S. Marines at War and at Home

The Devil and John Holmes - 25th Anniversary Author's Edition: And Other True Stories of Drugs, Porn and Murder

Janet's World: The Inside Story of Washington Post *Pulitzer Fabulist Janet Cooke*

Travels with Bassem: A Palestinian and a Jew Find Friendship in a War-Torn Land

The Lonely Hedonist: True Stories of Sex, Drugs, Dinosaurs and Peter Dinklage

Tattoos & Tequila: To Hell and Back with One of Rock's Most Notorious Frontmen

Shaman: The Mysterious Life and Impeccable Death of Carlos Castaneda

Hunting Marlon Brando: A True Story

A Boy and His Dog in Hell: And Other True Stories

The Rise and Fall of a Super Freak: And Other True Stories of Black Men Who Made History

The Pope of Pot: And Other True Stories of Marijuana and Related High Jinks

FICTION

Deviant Behavior, A Novel
High Tolerance, A Novel

TEMPLE OF DOOM

AND OTHER STORIES OF KIDS AND CRIME

BY MIKE SAGER

Cover design and cover art by WBYK.com.au
Interior design by Siori Kitajima, PatternBased.com

Cataloging-in-Publication data for this book
is available from the Library of Congress.
ISBN-13:
Paperback: 978-1-958861-34-9
eBook: 978-1-958861-33-2

Published by The Sager Group LLC
TheSagerGroup.net
In conjunction with NeoText
NeoTextCorp.com

TEMPLE OF DOOM

AND OTHER STORIES OF KIDS AND CRIME

BY MIKE SAGER

For Mitra
The best for last

CONTENTS

Kids who listen to Slayer are "violent and heavy drug users," says one expert. "The band members worship Satan," says another. All of which has had a predictable effect on the band's popularity. Perception meets reality.

TEMPLE
OF
DOOM

Police were baffled when eight Thai Buddhist monks and one nun were killed execution-style in a temple outside Phoenix—the worst mass murder in Arizona history. Nobody wanted to believe the crime had been committed by a pair of gung-ho ROTC students from the local high school.

I t was to be a special day at the temple, so Chawee Borders arrived early, a bouquet of flowers in her hands. August in Arizona, the flat valley west of Phoenix. By ten a.m. the temperature was already pushing triple digits. Chawee squinted into the blazing sun, shook her head, made a noise behind her teeth, *tsktsk*. Heat eddied through the rubber soles of her shoes: It felt like walking through a skillet. No matter how long she lived here, Chawee couldn't quite get over the idea that they called *this* the monsoon season. Baked earth and cotton fields, battered Chevys, migrant pickers, mountains rising in the distance, barren and craggy against a wan blue sky. Half a world away, in her native Thailand, it was also the season of monsoons, all lush and wet and green, the time of rains and contemplations, of Buddhist retreat.

In Thailand, it is said, there is a temple on every corner, and every summer, 1 percent of all males become monks. In Phoenix, there is only one temple, Wat Promkunaram, an L-shaped stucco building with a red ceramic roof on five acres of lonely scrub in the western part of Maricopa County. This year, two boys had entered the temple. Matthew Miller, 17, had just arrived. David Doody, 14, had just left. The celebration tonight was for them.

Along with Matthew, there were six monks, a nun, and a young acolyte living in the Wat. Matthew was the son of an American Air Force vet and his Thai wife. Born in Myrtle Beach, South Carolina, Matthew spoke Thai but had never been to Thailand. He was a friendly kid who played electric guitar, called his buddies "dude."

Cooked part-time in a Chinese restaurant. His nickname was GQ, earned for the thrift-store three-piece suits he painstakingly ironed and accessorized. None of the other kids wore suits to school. It was Matthew's own style, part of his need to be his own person. Half Thai, half American, he'd found something special in his difference, was in the teenage process of puzzling himself together with pieces from many worlds.

Lately, Matthew had become more curious about his roots, something his mother traced to his Grandma Foy. Foy Sripanpiaserf was a youthful seventy-one, one of the few mothers who had followed their daughters to America. Though she had learned to love hot Ovaltine and pro wrestling, she still spoke no English. After years of farming rice paddies, raising water buffalo and chickens along with children, picking her roots and vegetables from the ground free of charge, she found Phoenix a very strange place to live. She worried that when she died, her spirit would inhabit an English-speaking place, too.

The Temple was thus a great comfort to Grandma Foy; she spent most of her time there—cooking, cleaning, gossiping, giving advice. Often Matthew came along. It surprised no one this summer, when Grandma Foy declared her intention to become a nun, that Matthew decided to follow.

Matthew planned to stay in the temple about a month. He didn't want to spend his whole vacation sitting around acting holy, and this was fine with the abbot. When a man becomes a Buddhist monk, he can stay for a few weeks or a lifetime. He can leave and return. It is honorable to be a monk for any length of service; they are living icons of the highest spiritual pursuit.

The first monk was Guatama Buddha, a Hindu prince born in the sixth century B.C. Buddha understood life as a complete universe of endless rebirth, with many heavens above, many hells below, one lifetime affecting the next. Buddha taught that a person could build merit for his fortunes in each successive life by practicing right thoughts and good deeds, by keeping a pure heart. Beyond this, there is the ultimate reward, Nirvana. Reaching Nirvana, he said, entails study, meditation, simple labors, a removal from material concerns.

The key is coming to understand the truth: "The way things really are." When the truth becomes clear, suffering ends. The soul leaves the cycle of rebirth and rejoins the universe, much as a drop of water rejoins the ocean.

Being a practical religion, Buddhism recognizes that everyone can't be monk. For one thing, monks are celibate. For another, they're not supposed to cook or work for money. Most people, therefore, take for granted that other lifetimes are in store. Meanwhile, they seek karmic merit by serving the monks.

Since Chawee Borders lived right down the dirt road that led to the temple, she cooked lunch every day for the monks. Like Matthew's mother, like many of the women in a community of 2,000 Thais who settled in this unlikely outpost near Luke Air Force Base, Chawee was a Vietnam-era war bride. Beginning in the late sixties, the Thai population of Phoenix had burgeoned. GI brides, working-class families, professional men, they set up housekeeping and surgical practices, went to work in factories, opened restaurants and businesses. By 1983, the only thing missing was a temple. A committee of wives was formed. Letters were written to Thailand, requesting monks for a spiritual center. To raise money, the women sold eggrolls, hosted a beauty pageant, recycled cans. Finally, five years ago, Wat Promkunaram was built.

Now, on the morning of Saturday, August 10, 1991, Chawee shut her car door, walked with her friend Premchit Hash across the parking lot toward the temple kitchen. Just shy of the grass, the women stopped. The grounds were flooded. The monks hadn't turned off the irrigation. "Why would they forget?" Chawee wondered out loud. Premchit shrugged. Her arms were laden with trays of food. The two women circumnavigated, seeking a drier entrance.

At the east side, as was custom, they removed their shoes, stepped into the ceremonial hall. As Chawee padded toward the altar, she was struck by the silence. So quiet. The monks should have been up now for hours. But then again, she'd known the monks to sleep late. She put a finger to her lips, "Shhhhh," she urged Premchit, speaking in Thai, a language with no plurals. "The monk sleeping."

The monks were pampered and beloved figures, led by their abbot, Phra Maha Pairat Kanthong. Phra means something like Father or Reverend. Maha is a title denoting rank. Pairat, as he was called, was thirty-six years old. He'd been in Phoenix since the beginning of the Wat. To an American mind, he conjured the image of Spencer Tracy in *Boys Town*, known for his enthusiasm, his strength, his devotion to boxing, gardening, and TV news.

Though he liked to tease and laugh, some say Pairat was troubled. The congregation was thin, the coffers were low. The children, almost all of them half American, didn't attend very often. Sometimes, on Sundays, the congregation sparse, he almost despaired. He knew his concerns were earthly, unworthy for a monk. Yet still he worried—a human with responsibilities, a holy man, still a man.

As there were others under his charge, Pairat did his best to show a good face. Suthichai Annutaro, 32, was the eldest of a large family with a history of producing monks. Boonchuay Cahiyathammo, 37, was from Chang Mai, the poppy growing area in the north of Thailand known as part of the Golden Triangle, the heroin center of Asia. Somsak Sopha, 47, had lectured on Buddhism, worked among the hill tribesmen of Thailand, traveled to Taiwan, the Philippines, and Sri Lanka. Siang Mahapanyo, 28, was an artist, sculptor, inventor, and toy maker. Chalern Kittipattaro was twenty-nine. Little else about him was known. A monk can be collegial or choose to keep to himself. Like the rest, Chalern's main duty was to seek personal enlightenment, help others along the path.

Also under Pairat's care this summer was Chirasak Chirapong. Known affectionately as Boy, he was the abbot's nephew, 21, the longhaired son of a wealthy branch of his family. Chirasak had not entered the monkhood; he was just vacationing. He'd made friends with David Doody and with his older brother, Jonathan. The American Thai boys had turned him on to malls, Slurpees, Arnold the Terminator, *Boyz n the Hood*. Boy bragged of having more than $2,000 in a small safe in his room. He spent it freely, financing all the outings.

Now, on the morning of the celebration for the novices, Chawee placed her flowers on the altar, bowed to the six-foot brass and gold leaf Buddha. She and Premchit passed behind the altar, into the kitchen. They busied themselves unwrapping platters. Maybe the monks were outside somewhere. No doubt they'd be back soon.

Then the telephone rang. There was a pay phone right next to the kitchen. Chawee picked it up, heard a click, then silence. Thinking she might have answered the wrong phone, she walked out of the kitchen a few steps, over to the private line. The cord was cut.

Puzzled, Chawee turned, surveyed the living room. Over in the middle, beyond the sofa, she could see all the monks sleeping on the floor. She'd known the monks to sleep on the floor. It wasn't too unusual. But then she noticed someone wearing white. Nuns dressed in white. Grandma Foy was sleeping with the monks! This was *not* allowed.

"Wake up!" she called gently, "Wake up, my monk." She took a cautious step forward.

"My monk!"

Matthew, Boy, Grandma Foy, Pairat, the monks ...

All of them were dead.

It took three tries for the first officer on the scene to count the nine victims. "I guess it was mind-boggling," he would later say.

Within hours, Wat Promkunaram was cordoned all around with yellow crime scene tape. Inside more than two dozen police combed for clues, some wearing rubber boots against the copious blood flow. Other policemen—rubberneckers, top brass—trampled about, unwittingly contaminating evidence, what little there was: seventeen expended .22 caliber long-rifle shells, four expended yellow shotgun shells. Medical examiners would conclude that each of the nine had been shot execution style with the .22—at close range, above the base of the neck, while lying on his or her stomach. All except Boy had been shot twice. Several had superficial wounds from the birdshot. There had been no struggle. All nine had lain motionless, waiting to die, one at a time.

Though the ceremonial room was untouched, the living quarters had been ransacked. There were no usable fingerprints; the assailants had worn gloves. Police removed a section of wall on which the word

Bloods had been carved in two-foot letters. This information was kept mum, as was the curious evidence that someone had set off a fire extinguisher, sliced open a bag of rice, poured soda into Pairat's computer. Guarding such details is standard in police work. When a suspect mentions secret details, detectives know they have the right man.

In the coming weeks, a sixty-six-person task force would be assembled under the command of Maricopa County Sheriff Tom Agnos. The media were calling this the worst mass murder in state history, and Agnos—a gruff, chain-smoking good old boy serving his first elected term—was in charge. He coordinated personnel from local and state police agencies, the FBI, the Immigration and Naturalization Service, the DEA, even the Bangkok police. People around the world were watching in horror.

At first, police speculated that robbery was the motive, citing jewelry and ancient treasures kept in the temple. Then, upon learning that monks live in virtual poverty, they blamed Asian gangs. As each day passed, new theories were bandied about: It had been the work of a "lone psychopath," an "isolated bunch of kooks," a "Laotian mafia figure from Fresno," the KKK, a heroin trafficker.

Over the next two years, things would only get more complicated. What began as a gruesome, incomprehensible massacre of innocents would degenerate further over time into a complex, confusing, disturbing case that highlighted America's myriad ills: clashing cultures, fractured morals, family dysfunction, the tragically easy availability of firearms, the frightening latitude taken by law enforcement groups during increasingly martial times. In the end, the case of the murders at the Wat would become more than just another senseless tragedy. Some would say it was a sign.

For the first several weeks after the murders, police ran in circles. After 15,000 man-hours of investigation, they were clueless. Then lead No. 511 lit up the switchboard. The tipster said he had the scoop on the murders at the "Budapest" temple.

Three hours later, detectives pulled up to the Tucson Psychiatric Institute. There they met the tipster: a short, heavyset Mexican

American, twenty-five years old, "alert and eating a graham cracker," according to a police report. The tipster asked the detectives if they had found blood on the walls at the temple.

Bingo. The cops had found the word Bloods carved in two-foot letters. Michael Lawrence McGraw was brought in for questioning, advised of his rights. Waving his right to a counsel, he confessed, implicating himself and four others.

Acting swiftly, police made arrests. Sheriff Agnos held a press conference. Five arrests, five confessions, he told reporters. Case closed.

One week later, McGraw and the others recanted their confessions. "I had nothing to do with this," McGraw told the *Arizona Republic* in a jailhouse interview.

In the southside barrio of Tucson, a dusty patchwork of poverty, neighbors and relatives rallied in defense of their own. McGraw, they said, was known as Crazy Mike. According to a thirty-page probation file, McGraw had been arrested twice for false reporting of crimes. One counselor questioned McGraw's "discrimination of reality to fantasy." Said a longtime neighbor: "If the police had stopped to ask anyone about Michael, we would have told him."

Unfortunately, the police had not asked. They had obtained search warrants without consulting the county attorney. SWAT teams in black hoods broke down doors with battering rams, threw stun grenades into empty apartments. Not one shred of physical evidence was recovered from the suspects' homes.

Then it was announced that one of the confessed killers was to be released. The man worked at a greyhound track. Videotapes of races placed him atop the starting gate at the time of the crime.

Soon, defense attorneys began crying coercion. The ACLU concurred. The Tucson men, it was alleged, had been questioned for ten to twenty hours without a break. They had been denied food, sleep, lawyers, and phone calls. Some interrogations were taped, some were not. The men were shown a roomful of evidence from the temple—including pictures and crime-scene drawings—before they were questioned. All five men said that the police had threatened them with the gas chamber, with having their fingernails pulled out, with a lake and an anchor. A lawyer characterized the cops' technique as "World Wrestling Federation tag-team interrogation ... tantamount to a rubber hose."

Four of the men were bound over for trial.

"Okay, Jonathan, we're gonna go through this thing again," said Detective Rick Sinsabaugh, tired and exasperated in the ninth hour of interrogation. Sinsabaugh was a ten-year veteran of the Maricopa County Sheriff's Department, a long drink of water in cowboy boots. It was early in the morning of October 26, more than two months after the murders.

The kid across the table sobbed, then sniffled. His name was Jonathan Doody, the older brother of the novice monk David. He was dressed in a baby-blue ROTC uniform. He sat up a little, stared at the cop. Tears began to flow. "When you caught those people in Tucson, they were laughing at you! They had nothing to do with it!" he said.

"Who was laughing at us?" asked Sinsabaugh, outraged.

"They beat the system."

"Who?"

Jonathan cut his eyes to the floor. "Them," he mumbled.

Sinsabaugh sighed. "Listen, Jonathan," he said, his voice warming. "We're not going to be going out and telling people what you told us, okay? Come on, pal, join the team. Be a soldier, Jonathan. Come clean, my man. Hey! Jonathan! Look at me!"

Jonathan was seventeen. His mother, Laiad, was a regular at the temple, and Jonathan knew Pairat and Boy and all the rest. Though he was born in Thailand to a Thai father, and spoke English with an accent, Jonathan knew no Thai, had no interest in Buddhism. He'd been baptized in Valdosta, Georgia, by a Pentecostal minister. His nickname was LT, for lieutenant, his rank in the ROTC. He considered himself American.

Jonathan's stepfather was career Air Force; Jonathan wanted to become a pilot. In school, he was a gung-ho commander in the Air Force ROTC. On weekends, he maneuvered with the Civil Air Patrol.

He was quiet and serious, had a military bearing. He knew ROTC was his only chance for college. He studied hard, drilled hard, practiced good manners. In sum, he was seen by all who knew him as the model boy, the model immigrant, a throwback to the old ideal: that people could come to the land of the free, shed their old ways, assimilate, live out the American dream.

It was now the morning of October 26, more than two months after the murders. Last night, the Agua Fria High School Owls had a home football game, and Jonathan, as always, commanded the honor guard. After the anthem was played, Jonathan marched the squad off the field, and Sinsabaugh walked over and tapped him on the shoulder. Jonathan went quietly. He had no reason to do otherwise. He liked Sinsabaugh. Up till now, Sinsabaugh had been treating him like a fellow soldier—an inside agent who could help police solve this mess.

The file on Jonathan Andrew Doody had been opened inadvertently ten days after the murders. Police at Luke had stopped two cars, a silver Mustang and an orange Nova, for "suspicious activity." Jonathan had just bought the used 5.0. The Nova belonged to his friend Rolando Caratachea, known as Rollie. On the back seat of the Nova was Rollie's .22 caliber rifle. The police told him to stow the rifle in the trunk, then let him go.

Two weeks later, as cops on horseback and in helicopters combed the desert between Tucson and Phoenix, looking for the murder weapon, the Air Force called about Rollie's .22 rifle. Sinsabaugh later drove out to the base to see Rollie. He asked if he could borrow his .22 for routine testing, telling him it was part of a sweep for stolen arms. Since Rollie's mom had bought the gun on sale at Kmart for Christmas, he gave it up willingly. Sinsabaugh took the rifle to the lab, put it in line behind eighty other .22s to be tested.

That night, Lead No. 511 came in over the phone. The cops focused on Tucson. Rollie's rifle was forgotten.

Six weeks later, there was still no shred of physical evidence. The task force had become a nightmare of infighting, all of it followed closely by the press. Detectives were beginning to believe that the Tucson suspects were innocent. The top brass was clinging to their confessions. Detectives were being ordered to rewrite reports, according to news reports.

Then the lab got around to testing Rollie's Marlin .22. There it was. The murder weapon.

It didn't take much footwork to pinpoint Jonathan as a new suspect. Rollie had lent the gun on the weekend in question to Jonathan and another ROTC cadet, Alessandro Garcia, known as Alex. The exchange occurred outside a party; there were many witnesses. Likewise, on the night before the killings, Jonathan told his girlfriend that he was going to "play in a game" involving an "intrusion alert" near the temple. Another friend says that after the murders, Jonathan had bragged about killing the nine Buddhists on behalf of the Office of Special Investigations for the Air Force (OSI) because they were "invading national security and had to be eliminated." Jonathan had claimed he was a paid OSI sniper who'd killed the Thais "mercenary style." Once a person commits a mercenary killing, he said, "you will always see and hear the blood rushing from their heads."

Now, in what his attorney would later characterize as a "brutal, nonstop, fourteen-hour interrogation," teams of deputies implored, begged, beseeched, yelled at, and comforted Jonathan. They called on his patriotism, his sense of team spirit, his need to get things behind him. At one point, his attorney suggests, Sinsabaugh may have even "de-Mirandized" Jonathan when he said that the police "won't be going out and telling everybody what you told us."

Throughout the taped proceedings, Jonathan said as little as possible. The story that emerges from the seventeen forty-five-minute tapes—acquired through a source by *GQ*—sounds improvised, as if he were trying to please the cops, weaving together details that were fed to him.

Jonathan claimed that he and Alex had been approached by a friend of Rollie's, who was a member of a gang. The friend wanted help to breach the temple's security system, which consisted of two motion-detector lights in the parking lot.

Jonathan said he didn't know who shot whom or who had which gun. He didn't know the names or races of his accomplices. He could, however, describe the shots. He imitated them for the police, making the sounds like a kid playing war. *Pow, pow ...Pow, pow ...*

Afterward, Jonathan said, they all reconvened at a dry river bottom. The gang members warned Jonathan and Alex: If they talked they'd be "eliminated."

"While you were being fingerprinted, I asked you how you were doing. Do you recall that?"

"Yes, I do," said Alex Garcia, Jonathan's closest friend.

"And do you remember what you asked me?"

"I said, 'What's going to happen to me?'"

"Correct," said Detective Russ Kimball, reviewing their previous conversation, speaking not so much to the blanket-wrapped tenth-grader sitting across the table as he was to the hidden microphone. It was 8:00 a.m. on October 26, in an interrogation room next to the one in which Jonathan was being questioned. Kimball was recollecting a conversation he'd had with Alex a short while ago, attempting to get it onto the record.

"My recollection, Alex," said Kimball, pointing with his Mountblanc pen, "is that I said there was a possibility that you wouldn't go to jail. And you could .... what? Do you remember what I said?"

"Walk out."

"Walk out. Okay. At that point in time you asked me what?"

"I asked what if I told the complete story without any lies."

"Good, Alex, good!" said Kimball.

Five hours earlier, after questioning Jonathan for a while, police had obtained a search warrant and raided the Garcia house. Jonathan had been bunking with Alex since school began. Police were searching for several cameras, a flash, a boom box, a bullhorn, a pair of binoculars, a portable CD player, some gold leaf paper—items that had been taken from the temple. They found those things, along with a pair of air force snow boots and a Stevens Model 67 20-gauge shotgun, the other weapon used in the temple murders.

Two hours into his interrogation, at 5:33 a.m., Alex asked for a lawyer. The police called his father. Then they took Alex for mugs and fingerprints.

Presently, Juan Garcia arrived in a squad car. Before he saw his son, he talked to the detectives, their captain, even Sheriff Agnos. They offered him donuts, told him Alex was a good boy. They said Alex could tie the Tucson four to the murders. They mentioned a sentence of seven to nine years, a deal. If only Alex would talk.

Juan Garcia was shocked. As far as he knew, his son had never been in trouble. He baby-sat neighbors' kids, fixed bikes in his driveway. He was a smart boy who'd skipped seventh grade. Six-four and beefy, Alex was a lineman on the football team. "He was a Gentle Ben type," Juan would later say. "He would apologize when he hit someone too hard in practice."

Alex talked to his father several times. There was a lot of hugging and crying. Juan—himself six-six and nearly four hundred pounds—urged his son to tell the truth. "I love you, *mijo*," he said.

"I love you too, Daddy," Alex said.

Just after 8:00 a.m., the questioning began anew. Through the wall, Alex could hear Sinsabaugh screaming at Jonathan. The tape rolled. Alex began.

"It was just an idea that me and Jonathan ... Should I mention names?"

"Absolutely," said Kimball.

"... that Jonathan Doody had come up with. Basically for money. Because Jonathan was attempting to purchase a new car, a used Mustang 5.0. He needed $2,000, and Boy had said he had $2,000 in a little safe.

"To start out, we collected information from his brother. David, his younger brother, attended the temple. We asked, like, were there security cameras, there weren't any. Alarms, there weren't any. How many people were there, if they had weapons underneath their beds. And we just collected information and it came to the point of, well, that it was a go."

The boys drew a diagram, made a plan. Next they decided they needed guns. There were four rifles in Alex's house. He would take the shotgun kept in his father's closet. It was hidden. Juan wouldn't notice it missing. For Jonathan, they decided to ask Rollie to borrow his .22.

On Thursday, August 8, they got the rifle, a Marlin .22. That night, they went out into the desert to test it. They tried to fashion a silencer from a length of pipe and some bottle caps, following instructions from a book. Though the silencer worked, it was only good for two or three shots. They nixed the idea. For clothes, they decided on BDUs—battle dress uniforms or camouflage fatigues—along with web belts, knives, right angle flashlights, caps, bandannas, tank goggles: everything military issue, from either ROTC or Luke. And Air Force surplus snow boots. The boots were very large; they would leave oversized footprints, confuse the cops.

At 10:00 p.m. on Friday the boys turned onto Maryland Avenue, doused the headlights of the Mustang Jonathan had just picked up on credit from a friend. They turned right into the temple lot, synchronized their watches.

Double-time in a half squat, they ran to the nearest wall, worked their way around to the kitchen door, the west side.

Jonathan hit the door first. "Police!" he yelled.

The monks and the others were watching television. They were startled by the masked soldiers. "We told them to get on the floor, and we told them that, you know, we were here," Alex said.

Jonathan cut the phone line and went to the bedrooms. Alex could hear things breaking, shelves tossed, a lot of noise. After some time, Jonathan returned to the living room, and Alex went back through, making sure Jonathan didn't forget anything. Along the way, Alex came across a fire extinguisher. He'd always wanted to shoot one off, so he did, spraying foam around the hallway. He cut the bag of rice. Poured Coke into Pairat's computer. Then he carved the word Bloods on the wall in two-foot-high letters. *That'll throw a wrench in the works*, he thought. He packed the loot into two duffel bags.

When Alex returned, Jonathan was standing on a sofa, holding the gun on the prostrate monks.

"Then Jonathan said it was time to go," Alex told Kimball. "He said: 'No witnesses.'"

Kimball raised an eyebrow.

"Listen," Alex pleaded. "I'm being completely honest. I will sign anything. I will take a lie detector. This is true: I'm in the doorway, and he's on the couch, pointing the gun down at the monks, and he looks at me, you know, like, 'Go ahead, start.' And I just stood there, like, 'What do you mean?' And then I told him to come over here, I motioned him over. I told Jonathan that I didn't want to kill them. I seriously did not want to kill them. But he just said, 'No witnesses!' That was his exact words, 'No witnesses.'

"And he walked back to the monks and just started shooting, okay? And at that point of time I was like, something came over me, you know? I just stood in the doorway and kept pulling the trigger, pumping, pulling the trigger, until, you know, nothing was left. I don't know where I aimed. I just shot my four shots. Jonathan went around shooting the people in the back of the head with the .22 caliber, a couple of times to make sure that they were completely dead. He went from one to the next, kind of like *bang, bang .... bang, bang*, you know, like enough time between each to like aim at the head, just like a steady beat, not like *powpowpow*.

"It was just me and Jonathan. The four people in Tucson, they had nothing to do with it. *Nothing*. I don't know how they come about to the story. Rollie, nothing. We just used his gun. It was just me and Jonathan. No one else had anything to do with it."

The next night, October 26, Master Sgt. Brian Doody and the other members of his family—his wife, Laiad, his stepson, David, his bio-kids, Crystal and Michael—pulled into their driveway in a cherry red truck. It was a military-issue house at Maxwell Air Force Base in Colorado Springs, same as every other on the street, enlisted country. The Doodys had been living there—without Jonathan—since September 1.

Brian, 38, was a seventeen-year air force veteran, a munitions specialist who had recently cross-trained into satellites. He'd been raised in Connecticut, son of a construction truck driver. Always a loner, a bit of a nerd, Brian was scrawny and four-eyed growing up, the object of pranks and beatings. A few years after high school, his prospects dim, he joined the air force.

They sent him to Germany, where he serviced missiles. He began lifting weights, studying Tae Kwon Do. Two months in-country he was set up with Laiad on a blind date. She was the widow of a Thai. Her sister—a GI wife—had paid her way to Germany. The pair had been dating five months when her visa expired. There was only one thing to do. "She had it in mind to marry me. I guess I was the last to realize it," he says now.

Laiad had two sons, ages eight and five. They were living with their grandmother in a one-room house of corrugated tin in a village north of Bangkok. "The most excitement for the kids was waiting for it to rain so the dirt streets would fill up full of water and they'd take off all their clothes and go play in a puddle," recalls Brian.

Within two weeks of his wedding, Brian adopted the boys. Veerapol and Veeraphan Khan Kew became Jonathan and David Doody.

Once in Germany, Jonathan fixed on the fighter jets. There were F4s and F16s at the base. They'd take off trailing brilliant flames, bank low over the Doody house. Jonathan would squat for hours, Thai style on his haunches, watching the takeoffs, feeling the ground shake beneath him.

Within a year Crystal was born and the family was transferred to Valdosta, Georgia. The boys were put into public elementary school. Neither spoke English. They failed everything the first two years but were promoted anyway. Laiad spoke no English, didn't seem to want to learn. There they were, trying to make things work in a place where Asians were generally referred to as nips or gooks—and no one in the family could communicate. Laiad could speak to the boys but not to her husband. Brian had only a rudimentary knowledge of Thai. He carried his dictionary wherever they went. There was a language gap, a culture gap, a chasm. Brian despaired. He began drinking.

When Jonathan was thirteen, Brian was transferred to Guam. By this time Jonathan could read and write English. He refused to speak Thai at all. "Jon's and my relationship was really funny," says Brian, "maybe because he knew I wasn't his real father, even though he did call me Dad. A lot of things he did, I took personally. Like he'd spend all his time in his room. I felt it was against me, like, 'I'm gonna close the door so I won't have to look at Dad anymore.'"

Before long "Jonathan's hormones kicked in," Brian says. The distant boy became even more oblique. He found a first girlfriend, started staying out late at the base canteen with the other military brats.

"I'd tell him, 'Jonathan, be home by nine.' And he'd come home at ten-thirty. I would work myself up into a frenzy, just like a shark, you know? They'll tap at the meat and the more they tap the more they get excited. And that's the way I was. He'd get home late, and I'd ask him why, and he'd just stand there, no expression on his face at all. It would aggravate me more. And more and more. And finally I'd start grabbing and roughing him up. I used to hit him a lot. I used to slap him. I used the belt on him. Jonathan, he was total defiance. He wouldn't say one word. He'd just stare at me."

The wars continued until the Doodys arrived at Luke in the summer of 1989. The Civil Air Patrol had a unit on base; Jonathan immediately joined. In the fall he entered ROTC. Brian sought help for his abusive behavior, received counseling, and quit drinking.

"Jonathan changed overnight," Brian says. "He talked to me about things. I gave him books of mine, manuals and stuff. He was more mature, responsible, he did what I told him the first time I asked.

"It's like he'd found a place for himself. For all these years, especially in Georgia, he was so concerned about being accepted because his eyes were different, his skin was different, he had an accent. When he found ROTC he just found his niche. He was going to make a perfect military person because he loved America. He said, 'This is my land of opportunity.' He meant it."

Jonathan worked two jobs, rising before dawn to pedal five miles to McDonald's, then going to the base commissary after school to bag groceries. He gave all his earnings to his mom, who kept meticulous records on little slips of paper, stashed safely in a drawer with her underthings.

Soon after he got his driver's license, Jonathan went halves with his parents on a used Ford Escort. The head needed rebuilding. Brian envisioned it as a father-son project. Jonathan did not. He didn't want to learn how to work on his car. "Dad," he said, "someday I'll be able to afford people for that."

Goddamnit, thought Brian, *Jonathan was getting uppity.* He aspired to be an officer, a pilot—a class above his enlisted stepfather in the rigid caste system of the military. "Jonathan said, 'I'm gonna be better than you,'" Brian says. "It cut into my heart like a knife."

Then in early 1991, Brian announced his pending transfer to Colorado. Come September, he told his family, they would be gone from Phoenix.

As far as Jonathan was concerned, however, come September, he'd be a junior at Agua Fria High School, the commander of the ROTC honor guard. Up in Colorado Springs, the schools didn't have ROTC. He wasn't going. Period. There were fights. Big ones.

Brian left Phoenix for a month of training, returned just in time for the funerals of the temple victims. The family went together; Jonathan placed flowers and incense on each casket. To those around him, he seemed genuinely moved by the killings. He went back to the temple every day for a week afterward to help out.

At home, Jonathan wasn't quite so respectful. He was set on staying. Laiad was against the idea, but she helped him find an apartment, put down a deposit. Then she reminded him over and over that he was breaking her heart. Jonathan told Brian: "My friend says I could take you to court if you don't let me stay."

"I surprised him," says Brian. "I told him: 'Go ahead and get out now.'"

From mid-August until this October weekend, Jonathan had been living with Alex Garcia, sharing his bedroom. When Brian and the rest of the Doodys came inside, he noticed the telephone answering machine blinking. He hit play.

"Mr. Doody, this is the Durango Juvenile Detention Center. We have your son. He's been arrested on nine counts of murder."

One month later, November 20, 1991, *The Arizona Republic*:

"Maricopa County Attorney Rick Romley will ask Superior Court judges Friday to dismiss charges against four Tucson men held since September in the slaying of nine Buddhists monks."

"The sheriff just wouldn't accept the fact that the Tucson men and the Phoenix boys did not know each other," Romley said.

Following Alex's confession, he and Jonathan were booked on nine counts of robbery and murder. Rollie, after questioning and a lie detector test, was charged in two unrelated burglaries.

Weeks of controversy and political infighting ensued, culminating in the release of the Tucson Four. The men had been in custody for seventy days. They filed multimillion-dollar lawsuits. All except "Crazy Mike" McGraw. He went back to the Institute.

Time passed. The boys were judged to be adults for the trial, transferred from juvenile to county court. There were preliminary hearings, motions, legal maneuvers. Attorneys tried desperately to have the confessions thrown out, to uncover evidence and exhibits from the helter-skelter investigation, to overcome what felt to them like malicious prosecutorial zeal.

Eight months later, in July of 1992, Sheriff Agnos was still pushing his Tucson scenario. He even went so far as to visit Crazy Mike again. Mike told the sheriff that after the murders, he and the others had posed for a picture in front of the temple, with Mike holding up a newspaper to show the date. The photo, he said, was buried along with some ammunition, a watch, and a bag of rice on a butte outside Phoenix.

Agnos sent deputies up the mountain with picks and shovels. Nothing was recovered.

In November, Agnos was defeated by a landslide.

Alex Garcia shifted his weight in the hard metal chair, trying to get comfortable. He crooked his knees, slanted his legs to one side like a debutante from Miss Porter's, ankles kissing, foot shackles jangling against the concrete floor of the interview room. He held a pen awkwardly in his big fist, wrists cuffed, following each word of every sentence across the pages before him, lips moving ever so slightly to read.

Thick iron bars framed his face. From a three-quarter view he seemed handsome, with high cheekbones and almond-shaped eyes.

The jaw, thick and square, his father's, lent a sort of haughty, rakish air to the face of a teenage boy. From dead on, though, the impression was altered. You saw the stick-out ears, the chipped teeth, the meaty expanse of forehead; he appeared vaguely feral.

The document before him was a plea agreement. Though the police believed Alex's scenario, when it came right down to it, Alex was in bigger trouble than Jonathan. Courtroom justice is a game, with each side trying to win points inside carefully drawn boundaries, the rules of law and procedure. In the hands of the court, the narrative and nuance—the story of a complex happening—tends to get lost. Featured instead are tiny pieces of truth: singular details, items of evidence, shards. Those incriminated Alex.

The cops, in fact, had no hard evidence on Jonathan. He had confessed only to witnessing the murders. On Alex, they had his thumbprint on the shotgun, his air force boots. And they had the cameras and the other stolen property found in his bedroom. Though Jonathan was living with Alex, in legal terms, it was Alex's room. The goods were on Alex, even if he wasn't the shooter.

Alex was in trouble. He was the easier target in a big case with a freakish history and heavy ramifications, local and worldwide. And he was living in a Republican stronghold with a reputation out of the wild, wild west. A state with Mormon roots, cowboy sensibilities, an ever-growing population of Mexicans and foreigners of color, a reigning philosophy that seemed to mix Libertarianism with Prohibitionism. You could walk around Phoenix with a gun on your hip, go to a head shop and buy a crack pipe. Get caught using either, however, and you'd find Arizona's sentencing guidelines to be among the toughest in the nation.

Under Arizona law, complicity in an armed robbery is equal to pulling the trigger. Facing death by lethal injection, Alex made a deal—his testimony for his life.

So now he checked the pages carefully, asking questions of his lawyer, Luis Calvo, wondering if he was doing the right thing.

In the eleven or so months of their friendship, Alex and Jonathan had talked a lot about The Code. It is honored in the military, among thieves. It's about keeping your mouth shut. No one likes a snitch, especially not in jail.

But then again, in Alex's mind, he didn't pull the trigger. Fuck Jonathan. He was a comrade of interests for a time, sure. But mostly he was this funny, stupid, arrogant kid who couldn't pronounce the letter "r" and never put the "s's" on plurals—"*Come on, you guy, we go for a lide.*" He carried the instructional diagram from a package of condoms in his wallet. He seemed not to grasp exactly what was going on a lot of the time; he was always watching you to see what to do next. In sum, Jonathan was a dweeb, but he was also Alex's only friend with a license and a car. He would pick up Alex whenever he called. When you're sixteen, that's more than enough for friendship. But not enough to die for.

Reading through the agreement, Alex came to a clause that said he must state any knowledge of crimes committed prior to his arrest on October 25, 1991. Failure to disclose would void this deal, make him eligible for the death penalty without trial.

Alex read the clause again, then again. Finally he looked up. "Mr. Calvo?" he asked his attorney. "What if I know about another crime?"

As it turns out, Alex Garcia wasn't quite the Gentle Ben his parents knew.

As Alex tells it, in an exclusive jailhouse interview with *GQ*, he grew up hard, son of a repo man and a factory supervisor, "below average middle class." He'd lived his whole life in Maricopa County, in the West Valley. Suburban, exurban, rural in spots, the area has an equally eclectic population. There are snowbirds—so-named for their hair color and seasonal migrations—in retirement villages like Sun City; military housing around Luke; professionals in Litchfield Park; blue collars and farmers in Litchfield. Trailer camps for migrant workers; modest, ad-hoc developments of second and third generation Chicanos; apartments filled at dinnertime with a symphony of smells from Asia and the Middle East.

From the time he started elementary school—bussed each day to Litchfield Park, an affluent suburb nearby—Alex says he felt "like a poor boy, someone who wore the same clothes three days in a row and heard about it." Alex was a loner. "It was always like, 'What the fuck do I want to deal with them for, anyway?'" he says. He didn't need people or have the same interests as them. Then, as now, "I lived in my own mind," he says.

He did play with other kids sometimes, a group from the neighborhood. "We did a lot of shit," Alex says. "Like, there was this one house across the street, it was empty, and we just tore the shit out of it. I mean, I wanted to blow the damn thing up. Or we'd, you know, get sticks and our bikes and, what do you call that? Joust? We'd fly at each other down the street, try and knock each other off. I broke my arm from that.

"If you wanted to go somewhere where we lived, you walked or rode your bike. It wasn't 'Mom, take me here.' You walked. You didn't have malls, you didn't have three-wheelers or ATVs, so we made our own fun. We had the desert: Let's make a clubhouse. It was fun, but at the same time, it was hard because of the family situation. A bullshit lazy faggot for a father, a mother that works all the time, and a dick for a brother. I was the younger one. You know? The younger one gets beat? Well I got beat a lot of times. To me, it was like, fuck you, life's too short. I didn't want to be told what to do. I'd go where I wanted, I'd wear what I wanted. It was like, fuck it, you know?"

If Alex had his druthers, he would have been born earlier. "I'm a Vietnam freak," he says. His favorite movie is *Apocalypse Now*. He would have fucking fought. Jimi Hendrix on the tape player, humping an M60 through the slop, twin bandoliers of ammo across his chest. Vietnam: He would have fucking loved it. "It's the paranoia of not knowing," he says. "One second you can be sitting, the next you're dead. It's like, 'Hey, this shit's for real!'"

ROTC was thus a natural choice, though Alex would have preferred army or marine if they'd offered it. He met Jonathan the first day of freshman year. It was a perfect match: Alex the poor boy, the loner, the thinker; Jonathan the immigrant trying to blend in. Both of them had families from hell. Both were crazy for all things martial. They bonded instantly, an alliance of outsiders.

One night, at the beginning of summer vacation in 1991, the boys found themselves at a house party. There they met a new group of friends. One of them was Rollie Caratachea. He lived way out there in the boonies, had the distinction of being kicked out of his house and living in his car. He was said to have ties to the Avondale Barrio Locos, a Mexican drug gang. Altogether, there were like ten or fifteen of them hanging out in a knot at the party, drinking beer, goofing, everybody starting to get to know each other. As the night wore on, someone decided it was time to go to Sonic Burger.

"If you can imagine a Nova, a Mustang, a Camaro, and a little Ford Escort racing off down the road in a cloud of smoke, that's what it was," says Alex.

And so the summer took shape. "We did a lot of shit," says Alex.

The first thing they did was name themselves: AM Posse, for After Midnight. That was when the mischief always started. You could call the AM Posse a gang, though in times past you might have called it a frat or a club or an affinity group, a garage band, a softball team. All over Phoenix, all across America, nineties kids are forming posses or gangs or crews. Modeled upon the glorified media vision of the L.A. Crips and Bloods, they call themselves "posses" after the infamous Jamaican hoods, or maybe after Arsenio's band, or Ice Cube's homeys, or maybe just after the sheriff's vigilantes in the cowboy movies. Hybrid groupings, composed of kids of both genders, from different neighborhoods, all races and social strata, they organize not over traditional missions like turf or respect or drugs, but rather over the newer scourges of boredom and alienation.

Proliferating in cities and suburbs and rurals alike, what the members of these new-age gangs have in common is dysfunctional families. In this era of working parents, shifting values, societal chaos, the kids have no other choice but to go to each other. Today's kids find their structure, protection, opportunity, acceptance, love in the comfortable surrounds of their posse.

The AM Posse was also bonded by something else: a love of mischief and mayhem, violence and guns—the drugs of choice for the Just Say No Generation. "If you think about it," says Alex, "there's always something to get in trouble with. It's fun. It's free. It's living on the edge."

The AM Posse started out racing cars, laying rubber, doing donuts. When that got boring, they moved on to yanking stereos and siphoning gas, and then on to stealing cars. Jonathan and Alex liked to add military wrinkles. They'd patrol the perimeter, monitoring a police scanner. Counterintelligence, they called it.

Inevitably, guns came into the picture. Rollie had his .22 in the back seat. Others had guns of their own. They shot out streetlamps, pumped shotgun pellets into cars—drive-by assaults on inanimate objects. They kept doing car stereos, packing heat now for "protection." And then they moved on to "capers." Rollie and some others hit a mini-storage place twice. Another time, Alex, Jonathan, and Rollie went to rob a friend who had several large bottles of coins. They dressed in BDUs, each carrying a gun. The kid wasn't home. The mission was aborted. "It was like living in a movie," says Alex.

Guns have become a major problem in America, but in Arizona, where owning firearms has always been a way of life, they are "epidemic," experts say. In Phoenix, a kid can get a .22 pistol or a sawed-off shotgun for twenty-five dollars. For a little more he can buy a .38, for a little more a Mac 10 or a .9mm or an Uzi. Even in states with more restrictive gun laws, the black market thrives, with weapons being dealt out of car trunks and duffel bags. "Guns are magnetic," says Alex. "It's all about power. It's all about I've got control. You're gonna hit something if you aim at it. You're gonna blow it away. I like guns, I really do. I like knives too. I generally like weapons. Hell, if I could have got a .50 caliber machine gun in the back of a pickup truck, that would be cool."

There is something magical about guns and violence, Alex says. The American public seems to agree. Studies of television and movies have shown that by the time a child reaches eighteen, he has seen over 18,000 simulated murders, 100,000 acts of violence. Seventy percent of prime time TV programs include violence. The average home viewer witnesses sixteen violent acts a night. Children's programs have three times the amount of violence as adults'.

Witnessing so much feigned violence, a kid today has a sort of virtual reality experience with killing. Even if he's never held a gun, he's seen one used enough times that it seems second nature. Not surprisingly, the homicide rate among juveniles in America has more than doubled in the past decade.

"To me, what we were doing didn't seem wrong," says Alex. "I don't know, I'm weird with it. A lot of people would consider us, okay, a bunch of criminals. But what makes us criminals? If you get caught? Cause everybody does things wrong, everybody. To tell you the truth, we could have done a lot. We could have been the beginning of another kind of organized crime. We lived in a small community. We had several gun stores where we could have easily broken in. We had the houses out in the desert. Isolated settlements. We could have really made something of it."

By midsummer, however, the AM Posse had dissipated, and Jonathan and Alex were back on their own. For money, for something to do, they planned the temple caper. On August 9, 1991, they moved.

"You gotta imagine," says Alex, recalling the scene. "You got nine people, all laying face down with their hands clasped behind their heads. Every time a bullet hit, you know, every time the sound went off, you could just see them jerk. Like their body jerking. And then I remember the gurgling, the gurgling of blood in their throats. I wish I was a good enough artist to draw it. It's hard to put into words.

"The weird thing was the money, counting up the money and splitting it. We had a big grudge about it. We got I think $2,650. Jonathan owed $2,000 on the Mustang, and it was like he wanted to take that much and give me $650. Shit. I wasn't gonna play that. You're getting a fucking car, and I'm getting a couple shirts and a pair of shoes? Fuck that. We split it even. Then we went over to Circle K and bought Thirst Busters.

"To this day—you know, it's funny. You can pull a caper, and when you're there, you can say: 'Yeah, this looks right,' and then afterwards you're like: 'Why in the fuck did we do *this*?' That was the only thing: If we could have gotten rid of the .22, we could have, hell, we could have had robes, we could have had jars of blood in our closet, we could have had anything from the temple. As long as they didn't have the murder weapon. That's what caught us. We could have dumped it in the river, filed off the serial numbers, just thrown it on the street. We were stupid.

"There was a lot of mistakes. I shouldn't say I'm sad, but it's kind of fucked up. I mean, right now, after my case and everything, I could write a guidebook about how not to get caught. You could follow my handwriting and do all the crimes that you wanted.

"To tell you the truth, if me and Jonathan couldn't have been caught, I think there would have been more crime. I know for a fact there would have been. A lot more crime. A lot more murders."

"All right now, Alex. Are you ready?"

Deputy County Attorney Kenneth C. Scull was a distinguished veteran with a sculpted gray beard. He removed his glasses, rubbed his tired blue eyes. It was the first week of February 1993. He'd been working the temple case since the beginning, seventeen months before. Now Alex had asked for this meeting. There was something on his conscience that he wanted to say.

Shifting in his chair, Alex began his story. It began inside of a pickup truck in the sand dunes near the White Tank Mountains. Alex was at the wheel. Michelle Hoover was in the passenger seat. It was October 14, 1991, ten days before Alex and Jonathan had been arrested.

"So what do we do, Alex?" Michelle asked. She was fourteen, a freshman, less than five feet tall, the biggest love Alex had ever had. The pickup belonged to her mother. They were stuck in the sand, it was a school night, after three in the morning.

Alex slumped in the seat, stared out the windshield. The sky was black, freckled with a million stars. Michelle had a million freckles across her nose, beautiful blue eyes, fine long reddish hair with a new perm, the front moussed and standing up off her forehead. In the glow of the dashboard, she looked scared.

"Can you call your father?" asked Alex. "He can tow us out."

"Oh no! He's asleep." Said Michelle. "He'd kill me!"

In fact, Ted Hoover had never raised his voice to his daughter. She was an only child, a tomboy, an honor student, Daddy's pet.

When she was born, six years into their marriage, Ted quit his job as a cop to spend more time with his family.

The Hoovers lived in affluent Litchfield. They had four Dobermans, a good piece of land. Ted was a boss in a big construction firm in the West Valley. Mom Kathy worked there too. Their daughter was known by all to be responsible, artistic, sweet, "one of those few people who's a saint." She took ballet and tumbling, was fair skinned, tended to be heavy. She liked Troll dolls, the New Kids on the Block, going to the mall, eating. Summers she taught Bible school.

Michelle had just entered ninth grade at Agua Fria. The first week of school, one day after class, her friend Liz invited her to watch ROTC practice. Liz had a crush on this guy Alex.

Liz's plans went slightly awry. When Alex met Michelle, "there was an instant flame," says Alex. "She was outgoing, she was funny, she was bursting with energy." He gave her his number, and she called that night. "He was scared because he thought his girlfriend was pregnant," says Michelle. "We talked and I just said it would be okay. And then he found out she wasn't pregnant, and he started talking to me more. And then he picked me over her."

The kids became close, very close. Closer than they'd ever been to anyone. For Michelle, it was her first boyfriend. And Alex—he'd never had someone like her. She came to ROTC practice every day. When they got home, they talked on the phone before and after dinner, late into the night, also the first thing each morning.

Michelle began to change. She wore makeup, fussed with her clothes, went on a starvation diet. Kathy would tell her to get off the phone and find her on again five minutes later. She no longer did her chores, had no interest in clubs or events. Kathy never met the Garcias, nor did they ever offer to carpool.

As the Hoovers saw it, Alex was the love interest from the other side of the tracks. In his days as a cop, he said, Ted had seen how Mexican men treated their wives; he wasn't happy with this at all. But the Hoovers didn't say much. What could they say? Michelle was head over heels. "I was drawn to him," says Michelle. "On a scale of one to ten, it was a ten, you know. I cared so much about him."

At midnight on October 14, while Ted and Kathy slept, Michelle and Alex were cooing to each other from the phones in their respective bedrooms. They'd been dating for three weeks now; this was their custom, watching TV together, giggling, declaring their love. Sometime during the conversation, Alex suggested that Michelle commandeer her mom's truck and pick him up. Though the fourteen-year-old had no license, she'd been driving with her parents in the car for years. She was due to take drag racing lessons next summer. Michelle was hesitant.

"If you love me you'll do it," Alex told her.

"I do love you," said Michelle, "but it's a school night."

Eventually, Michelle assented. They made a plan: Michelle would take her dad's .9mm semiauto and his .22 magnum, steal outside to the truck. Underway, she'd call Alex from the car phone and let it ring once, his signal to jump out his bedroom window with his brother's .22 rifle. They'd go shooting out at White Tanks Mountain.

Michelle picked up Alex, drove out to the dunes, parked, and left the headlights on so they could see what they were shooting. For targets Alex had brought along a plywood board and a stolen motorcycle helmet. When they got tired of shooting, Michelle let Alex drive around the dunes. Now they were buried up to the hubs. Michelle was scared, worried that her parents would be worried. On the other hand, this was a grand adventure with the boy she loved. She knew she shouldn't be there, but it felt right.

"It's funny," Alex says. "In my mind I'm saying, 'Come on, you're sixteen, you've got this girl that likes you, let's try and do something. Let's have sex.' But on the other hand I'm saying, 'Fuck no! I'm not doing that to her.' With some girls, it's only sexual. But I liked who she was. I mean, here you've got a guy who does what he wants when he wants, and he's got to live for himself. But then you get a girl that you really need, that you really like—It's weird how that shit works."

At daybreak the kids dug out, drove to Alex's house. He stole money from his mother, gathered up his BDUs and some camping supplies. They hit the road, on the run, north toward Horseshoe Dam.

After stopping at a mini-mart to buy provisions, Alex pulled into the Mesquite Campground in Northern Arizona. They found a spot, built a fire, slept in the bed of the truck. For the next two days they hung out, walked, talked. They discussed sex, but Michelle said she wasn't ready. Alex didn't press. They were having fun. The campground was empty except for a nice hippie lady and a crazy guy, like a homeless vet, all shaggy and dirty with a beard.

On the third night, Alex asked Michelle if she wanted to go home. She said she did but didn't. She was confused. "I tried, you know, to act happy around him and I was happy," says Michelle. "But I knew I should be home. I was hoping the police would find us."

Even if Michelle had wanted to go home, they had a problem: They were out of gas, money, and food.

"We're gonna have to rob somebody," Alex said.

The hippie woman was the obvious target. She was camping right near the Verde River, a secluded spot. Before it got dark, Michelle went over to her site to ask for matches, to case her out. "She's a nice lady," Michelle reported.

In fact, many people thought Alice Cameron was a very nice lady. Fifty years old, Alice was a little kooky, a kind of hippie holdover. She'd married a divorced man with children and raised them like her own, then split. A gifted paralegal, she'd freelanced for many Phoenix attorneys over the years, turning down dozens of offers of full-time work. She's had no contact with her birth family or her married family for fifteen years. She was a free spirit dressed in flowing clothes, working just enough to finance her next walkabout.

"We're gonna have to kill her," Alex told Michelle. "No witnesses, you know what I mean?"

"I guess," said Michelle.

"Do you want to do it?" asked Alex.

Michelle looked up at Alex. It's not like she was surprised or anything. He had told her about the temple. He talked all the time about doing crimes. She wondered if he'd kill her too. She didn't say anything.

"If you love me you'll do it," urged Alex.

At around 1:00 a.m. on October 17, Alex and Michelle walked to the woman's campsite, Alex sticking to the tree line with his brother's .22 rifle, Michelle walking out in the open on the path. They found Alice reading in a chair on the bed of her pickup. Her back was to Michelle.

Michelle hesitated, looked over at Alex. He had the .22 shouldered and aimed, his finger on the trigger. He nodded.

She fired her dad's .9mm. She shot twice—*pow pow*.

Alice was toppled by the blasts. She screamed and kicked.

Michelle dropped the gun. She got very cold, began shaking uncontrollably. She turned her back and crumpled to the ground.

Alex ran to the truck, jumped up into the bed. He jammed a scarf into Alice's mouth, told her to shut up. "Hold her down!" he told Michelle.

Michelle climbed into the truck, held Alice's legs. She told Alice to calm down, that everything would be all right. Then she got Alex to help her wrap the woman in a sheepskin blanket. Alice quieted and Michelle took her hand.

Alice was bleeding heavily. Michelle was a pretty good shot: two bullets, two hits. Alice asked Michelle to get help. Michelle said she was sorry, she couldn't.

Almost two hours later, still in the truck, still bleeding, Alice looked up at Michelle. She seemed calm, serene. "I forgive you," she said. Then she died.

Now Alex and Michelle wiped down Alice's truck for fingerprints, ran back to their own truck with the loot: a bank card, four good-luck stones, a one-dollar bill, fifty-nine cents. As they drove away, Alex threw the stones out the window. A clerk in a gas station confiscated the card.

Police found them a few days later at a cabin not far away, owned by Michelle's cousins. Their parents were called. They never saw each other again.

"And how do you feel about Michelle now?" asked the county attorney, K.C. Scrull. He was visibly shaken.

Alex was pale and drained. "I'd rather not say."

"Why are you doing this?"

Alex looked at him. Why was he doing it? He didn't know. *Fuck! Stupid!* He was already sorry. Why did he rat out Michelle? He still loved her. A lot. He still had a picture of her; he still had one of her ponytail bands. "To protect my ass," he finally said.

"Okay, that will be all," said K.C. He closed his files, gathered his papers. He was in a hurry. There was a major mess to clear up.

Just after Alice's murder, police had arrested the shaggy Vietnam vet who'd been living at the campground. George Peterson, 46, was an ex-marine. He'd been hospitalized thirteen times for mental illness.

Peterson had endured only three hours of police interrogation before he confessed to killing Alice Cameron.

He had spent the last fourteen months in jail.

It is to be a special day at the temple, so Chawee Borders arrives early, a bouquet of flowers in her hands. It is August in Arizona, monsoon season, the time of Buddhist retreat.

Two years ago, nine Thai Buddhists had left their earthly lives in a senseless, bloody massacre: Pairat, five monks, Boy, Matthew Miller, Grandma Foy. This afternoon, the anniversary, the congregation will gather for a special ceremony; eight sets of ashes will be sealed into a monument on the grounds of Wat Promkunaram. The ninth set, belonging to Boy, was sprinkled by his parents over a river in Thailand.

Just about the time Alex was telling the county attorneys what he knew about Michelle, six new monks had boarded a flight in Bangkok, bound for Phoenix. One congregant, a western convert named Peter Angel, arrived at the temple just in time.

"They were obviously tired, very disoriented, they'd flown all the way nonstop," says Angel. "They got out of the van, filed directly into the temple, started chanting. They kept that up for like a half hour, then stopped. Then they all turned around in their places and looked at the people. It was beautiful, so wonderful. The people had been waiting so long for them to come. We didn't know their names or anything. But they were here."

There is a wall now around the grounds of the temple, an alarm system, bars on the windows and doors, a German shepherd. There are two portable cellular phones, one always recharging. And walkie-talkies. When a monk goes outside to work in the garden, he remains in constant touch.

To this day there are some in the temple who say the monks "died bad," that hanky-panky was going on. Sometimes—when a stiff breeze blows, when the lights blink, when Pairat's cat spontaneously arches its back and purrs like it's being stroked—some members of the temple say that the dead monks are trying to speak. Likewise Von Miller: Mathew's mother, Grandma Foy's daughter. One morning, she woke up to Grandma Foy, sitting on the bed, patting her leg, asking for a hot cup of Ovaltine. Mrs. Miller has stopped going to temple. It is said she is not well.

Mostly, the people in the congregation are trying to live the Buddhist way, in the present. They have gotten to know their new monks, special men themselves. Wenai, who learned English entirely from watching soap operas and cartoons, is now taking courses at the local college. Boontechr, the youngest, can fix anything. And Supab? An older man who speaks no English at all, he saw the other monks getting driver's licenses and wanted one himself. He got the manual, turned to the sample questions, memorized each one by sight. He scored 100 percent on the test.

The attendance has grown at services, births, and weddings, and special occasions go on. The people will always remember their first monks, but they are trying to forget the events of two years ago. They are trying not to feel anger or hatred. They are trying not to wish for revenge. In the end, said the Buddha, one gets what one deserves, good or bad. And indeed, the waters have been leveled. Misfortune has visited; the perpetrators of the ghastly happenings at the Wat have become victims themselves, justice having prevailed. Killing a Buddhist monk is one of Buddhism's five unforgiveable sins; the penalty is many lifetimes of suffering.

In July 1993, after a three-month trial as strange and convoluted as could be expected, Jonathan Doody was found guilty of nine counts of murder. His attorney, Peter Balkan, argued that Jonathan was an unwitting accessory to the murders, that he had been duped by others into participating in what he believed was a military exercise, not a robbery. Over and over at trial, Balkan sought to convince the jury that Rollie Caratachea was the gunman. It was, after all, his gun. He was said to never lend it out. He had gang connections, a record. Balkan's artful work was aided inadvertently by the zeal of the judge and prosecutor: Indeed, it seemed at intervals to observers that the case had been rigged against the boy. Time and again, defense evidence and testimony was ruled inadmissible. Balkan called for a mistrial on more than twenty occasions. A great deal of sentiment was created in the courtroom for Jonathan, more mature now, beefy and thick necked with bad skin, a close-cropped haircut. For his part, Jonathan sat impassively throughout the trial, showing emotion only when Alex testified. Then the change was remarkable. He narrowed his eyes, glowered at his former best friend, diddling a ballpoint pen so fast between the first two fingers of his right hand that it blurred.

Despite the procedural handicaps, Balkan managed to create enough doubt that the jury found Jonathan guilty of felony murder instead of premeditated murder, a lesser charge, but still one that carries the possibility of the death penalty. Jonathan's sentencing is scheduled for early January. Life without parole; death by lethal injection: His fate up to the judge.

Like the jury, psychologists who have interviewed Jonathan have questions about his involvement, and some also believe that Alex and Rollie may have played larger roles. They have found Jonathan to be deferential, respectful, "stereotypically Asian in his total lack of ability to emote or be demonstrative." Though news reports characterized Jonathan as being without remorse, these experts say that, in fact, Jonathan lacks the cultural vocabulary to show remorse, or even to explain himself, though he may indeed feel remorseful. They found his English and his knowledge of American society and convention to be almost nil. "A lot of the time," says one, "he just doesn't get it. He doesn't have a clue what's going on."

Still, along with these doubts and sentiments are certain irrefutable facts. If Jonathan was a hapless accomplice, would he have come away with half of the loot? Why would Alex protect Rollie? And why didn't Jonathan's attorney put him on the stand to tell the jury, simply, "I didn't do it."

If indeed Jonathan was the killer, say the psychologists, then what occurred that night at the Wat was a terrible splintering of his personality, a break from reality, from his normal function. Certainly the foundational fractures were there. The trauma of his real father's sudden death; his mother's disappearance to Germany; his change of name; his transplantation to a new culture; the constant moves to strange places like Valdosta and Guam; the lack of understanding of American language and culture; his militaristic, abusive stepfather; his guilty, isolated, passive-aggressive mother.

"If he did do it, it was because he totally freaked," said a psychologist who has interviewed all of the Doodys. "Something went awry in the boys' plan, and Jonathan just lost it, went into some other mode. He withdrew into a corner of his being that no one will ever get to. We'll never know for sure."

Asked by the psychologist what he thought would be his fate, Jonathan said, so quietly he could barely be heard, "Death penalty."

And what of all the rest?

Brian and Laiad Doody maintain their son's innocence. They have instituted a letter-writing campaign, have won the affections of the head monk in Los Angeles. Laiad has been back to the temple, has made her peace with the monks and her old friends. She was not forgiven; there was no need, for there was no blame. It was not her fault—deep in her heart, she can't entirely believe that to be true.

Brian Doody is thinking of mustering out of the air force early, even if it means a much smaller pension. In the military, a man is the commander of his dependents. If his family screws up, he is responsible. Master Sgt. B. Doody is the stepfather of a mass murderer, the worst in Arizona state history. No one will let him forget. He, too, is plagued with guilt.

Alex Garcia will be sentenced shortly after Jonathan. He faces twenty-five to 271 years. Alex regrets his decision to rat out Michelle. Of greater regret, perhaps, is his standing among inmates as a snitch. He's in segregation, must move about the prison under the protection of three guards. Jonathan, in the twisted world of cons, has come off cool: A mass murderer commands respect. As he would have made a fine soldier, so he makes a model prisoner.

Michelle Hoover, after a horrible year of silence and inner turmoil, copped a plea, full of remorse. She is currently serving fifteen years. Her dad, meanwhile, has undergone bypass surgery. Her mom has been diagnosed with multiple sclerosis. It is likely both will die before Michelle's release.

Sheriff Agnos remains in retirement. The new sheriff has ordered a review of all confessions, as well as an independent investigation of the entire temple investigation. Captain Jerry White, the commander in charge, has been reassigned to transportation. Detective Rick Sinsabaugh has left the force to become a probation officer. Detective Russ Kimball, the sergeant in charge, has been banished to uniform patrol, midnight shift.

Now, at the temple, the chanting and the prayers for the dead are about to begin. Pete Angel, a member of the Wat, says it doesn't matter who is guilty of the murders. "Things like this are expected," he says.

"As long as there are people on this earth, the world will be full of suffering and greed," says Pete. "Maybe in America it is a little worse. A nation of children and their evil toys. A complex society, full of complex rationalizations.

"You see, the Buddha looked at the world in very simple terms. He saw the answers in simple terms. Right thoughts, good deeds, a pure heart. To care instead of kill. To tell the truth. To love. To give people a break. To eschew violence and revenge and greed. To live and let live, to give all people their due. This is the Buddhist way. It is the only way. It is something that people must learn."

THE
DEATH OF
A HIGH
SCHOOL
NARC

The citizens of Midlothian, Texas, cared deeply about their town; development was coming, the future looked bright. Then the city manager decided there was a drug problem at the local school. What happened when the War on Drugs went horribly wrong.

I t was cool that Friday, the sun just gone, the night settling in upon the prairie. Midway between the towns of Venus and Midlothian, a brown-on-tan pickup juddered down a two-lane, a blond-haired boy at the wheel. He drove past fences and cattle, past fields of stubble and hay, up a rise and then down. It was eight miles from Midlothian to Venus. So far, he had covered the distance three times. Now, outside Venus, he slowed, signaled, turned around again.

This is stupid, Jonathan Jobe was thinking. Why the hell are you down here? Driving around in the dark, in the cold and the drizzle. You know that nothing's going to happen. There's no way they're gonna be down here.

North now on Highway 67, back toward Midlothian, the place Jonathan had lived all his life, where his parents had lived all their lives, a jumbled little town of 7,000 at a crossing of two railroads and two highways. It was also a town that was about to lose its innocence, though at the moment, at 7:30 p.m. on Friday, October 23, 1987, no one hereabouts suspected. As always, Jonathan could see in the distance the ghost skyline of the cement plant. It rose from the flat black of the north Texas plain, obscuring the stars, looking to him like a postcard of a big city, but really just a tease, a shimmering mirage above the town that the chamber of commerce called the Cement Capital of Texas, that the kids called Middle of the Ocean.

Jonathan checked his rearview mirror, then his watch. The wipers squeegeed across the windshield. He dialed the radio across the frequencies—static, commercial, strings, twang—and then he gave up, slotted a tape by a heavy-metal band called Slayer.

He'd installed the tape deck first thing after buying the 1979 Chevy Scottsdale, or rather Greg Knighten had installed it for him. Jonathan and Greg were neighbors. Back in the summer, when they were both fifteen, they had hung out together all the time. Then Jonathan turned sixteen. He got his license and his truck. Greg installed the stereo, tuned the engine, lubed the chassis. For a while, Jonathan drove him everywhere. Then school started and Jonathan met Richard Goeglein.

Jonathan and Richard took homemaking class together. They sat in the back of the room, on the right. Richard was funny. Richard was weird. One time he wrote, "What are you looking at, Dick-nose?" on the cover of his notebook and held it up in class. Everyone laughed so hard the teacher had to stop the lesson on color coordination and sentence the students to thirty minutes of "quiet time." Richard wore a pentagram around his neck; he told people he worshiped the devil. Sometimes he'd prick his finger and draw pictures with his blood. Richard could make his face rubber and do all kinds of accents, and he could draw anything, and almost from the day he and Jonathan met, it was Richard riding everywhere, Greg left behind at home.

Richard, 17, turned Jonathan on to Slayer and other heavy-metal bands, and the two were always together, talking mostly about bands like Anthrax and Metallica and Iron Maiden. Sometimes they played with a small, black, heart-shaped Ouija that Richard called Terry's Heart. Richard carried Terry with him everywhere he went. It was homemade of black plastic, sort of like the kind Milton Bradley sells. Sometimes when he was getting high, Richard would blow smoke on Terry and tell it, "I'm gonna get you stoned."

Some of the kids at school heard Richard explain that Terry was a dead girl and that the Ouija carried her "essence." The story was hazy, but apparently Richard had to find a girlfriend, and if he was with her for a year, she would change into Terry. Not change physically. She would take on Terry's "attitude."

The police in Williams, Arizona—a town of 3,000 near the Grand Canyon where Richard had lived before moving to Midlothian—would later speculate that Terry could have been Angelina Estrada, a girl about Richard's age who died in 1983. One rowdy night, the police say, Angelina was at a party. When someone threw a rock through the window, Angelina dropped dead. The cause was said to be heart failure.

Sometimes when Jonathan and Richard were together, Richard would set Terry on a table, press his fingertips to the edge, then close his eyes. In a few moments, Terry's Heart would move, all by itself, in figure eights. Jonathan saw this. Some other kids saw this. All by itself, it moved in figure eights.

Anyway, Jonathan began dating Richard's sister, Becky. Richard, in turn, fell in like with Jonathan's best girl friend, Gina. The night before, Thursday, Richard had kissed Gina for the first time. It had taken him a long while, six weeks if you start counting from their first encounter, which was also in homemaking. One day, Gina had stretched and accidently hit Richard in the head, and he had exclaimed, "Hey, what's up, bitch?" She turned around, angry. That's when she noticed his "meltin' blue eyes."

Even before the kiss, Richard and Gina and Jonathan and Becky had formed their own little clique. They didn't consider themselves dopers, ropers, or preppies, the recognized categories of kids at Midlothian High. Instead, they called themselves thrashers. The thrashers' music was hardcore, but their habits were not. Once in a while they smoked dope, but considering how little else there was to do in Midlothian, the thrashers were, as a group, pretty straight-arrow, especially compared with the dopers, who got high at least every weekend. Mostly they spent their time cruising and laughing in Jonathan's truck.

As it was, four kids across the front bench of the pickup was tight, and there was no room left for Greg. Kids being the way they are, it didn't occur to Jonathan that this was a big deal. They still saw Greg more than enough anyway, at school and around town. Besides, Jonathan and Richard were much closer than Jonathan and Greg had ever been. They were together day and night. They had plans to get an apartment the next summer and to party together for the rest of their lives. In early October, Richard and Jonathan made themselves brothers. Each boy cut a two-inch slit in the meat of the other's thumb, and then the two of them pressed their hands together, mingling their blood.

This Friday, an hour earlier, Jonathan, Richard, and Greg had met in Greg's bedroom. There was Marlboro smoke in the room, and the air was thick with alarm and raw nerves and indecision. As usual, Greg was begging.

It seemed that the rail-thin lad was always begging for something, most often for a ride. He had to go to Dallas to score dope. He had to go see his girlfriend, Jamie. He had to come along, just to come. This time, he was begging for something else.

"No way, man," said Richard. "I ain't going with you to do that shit."

"Man, he probably won't do nothing anyway," said Jonathan. "You know how he is."

"Yeah?" said Greg, rising up to his full sixty-eight inches. "That's what *you* think. I'm gonna do it. You can be sure of that."

"Damn, man," said Richard. "I ain't going *nowhere* with you."

"Come on, dude, *please!*" said Greg. "I got to have you down there. If you'll do this, I'll never ask you to do anything else again. I promise."

Richard looked at Jonathan. He looked at Greg. Then he said, "Okay, dude, if it means that much to you just for me to go down there, I'll go down there."

And so it was that a horn honked outside the house, and Richard and Greg went out the front door and got into a red GMC truck driven by a senior they knew as George Moore. Jonathan went out the back door and then toward Venus, with instructions to drive back and forth until about eight, when he would pick up his two friends along Farm Road 875.

This being a Friday in the fall, Jonathan knew that a lot of the kids would be over in nearby Red Oak, watching the Midlothian Panthers play the Red Oak Hawks. Neither the dopers nor the thrashers ever attended the games or any school activities that weren't required. There were too many rules.

The truth is, they had rules for just about everything at Midlothian High. The student handbook was eighty-three pages long. Printed blue and white, the school colors, the book enumerated, in extremely fine detail, dictums concerning hair length, metal shoe taps, suspenders, discipline classes, bus etiquette, delivery of balloons, facial hair, dress, earrings, parking, driving. On page eleven, the Pregnant Homebound program was explained. According to one teacher, twelve Midlothian High girls qualified for that program during the 1986-87 school year.

There was also the Just Say No program and the Student Assistance Program. SAP was a committee of teachers and administrators who sat in judgment of students. If a student was showing behavioral changes of any sort, a teacher could fill out a checklist and submit it to the committee. The committee would then hand out more checklists to teachers who knew the student. After evaluating the secondary reports, the committee would call the student's parents.

So the dopers and the thrashers steered clear of school events, and that was pretty much okay with everyone, because the preppies and the ropers didn't like the dopers, and the dopers thought the preppies and the ropers were symbolic of everything that was wrong with their school and their town. "They call us the problem kids," said one doper, "but I see the kids who are clean, and I see they're the ones with the problem. They're too hung up on society. I'm sixteen, you know?"

As Jonathan drove, he thought about school and the dopers and the thrashers for a while, trying to keep his mind off the plan, but his thoughts kept drifting back to George Moore, the kid who'd picked up Richard and Greg almost an hour before. Things, he had to admit, were adding up.

George was new to school, and he seemed all right at first, shy like a new kid, eager but not too eager to make friends. But as time went on and he started hanging out with Greg all the time, it began to be apparent that something wasn't right.

George's truck, a cherry red, step-side 1986 GMC pickup was too nice for a high school kid. The truck had a great stereo, but George never had it on. You had to ask. He always had money, but he didn't have a job. He said he lived with his uncle in Midlothian, but nobody ever went to his house, and you rarely saw him on weekends. He bought cigarettes, but he didn't inhale; the ashtray in his truck was spotless. George's wallet was weird too. All he had in it was his license and his money. There were no pictures of friends, no phone numbers, no scraps of paper. And George wore the kind of clothes a father wears. He always wore a polo shirt, blue jeans, a blue windbreaker—it seemed he was wearing a uniform. He always had a five o'clock shadow by three.

He did buy dope, though, lots of it. Come Friday night, the average doper would have maybe ten dollars in his pocket; it always took a few partners to buy a quarter-ounce bag of marijuana. George, however, always bought at least two, or two quarter-gram bags of powdered amphetamine—fifty dollars' worth. Plus, George was always driving Greg to Polk Street, the curbside drug market in Dallas, but he would never ask for gas money. One night he round-tripped with Greg, then round-tripped with another doper. Both times he bought dope.

When it came to smoking the pot he bought, well, George acted strange. He made these raucous sucking noises, but he didn't blow out any smoke. And then there were the allegations.

Once, George went to a doper's house, and when he left, the doper's father—a former doper himself—said George looked like a narc. Jamie's mother, who worked at the post office, said she'd heard that there was a narc in school and that his name was George. Cynthia Fedrick, a twenty-three-year-old cashier who let the dopers party at her apartment, said she didn't like the look of George. Another doper, who'd ripped George off for fifty dollars, reported that he had swung on George—smacked him right in the face—and that George had not fought back. Word also began to filter back from Polk Street: Dealers were getting busted after selling to George's red truck.

Then, on Wednesday night, two nights before, Greg and George had stopped at Cynthia's to smoke some dope. On a table was an expensive stereo. Cynthia had two kids, few clothes, and an ugly blue '69 Plymouth Valiant that she had bought for fifty dollars. She had just lost her job at the Road Runner convenience store; she never had much money. Everyone knew the stereo was hot.

The next afternoon, Thursday, the police came to Cynthia's apartment. They confiscated the stereo.

That was it: Greg and Cynthia and the others were now sure. George Moore was a student goody-goody who was telling the police what was going on in town.

They were almost right.

Now, traveling north on Highway 67, Jonathan took a hard right turn, and the tires spewed gravel. He headed east onto Farm Road 875, toward Mountain Peak.

You're gonna get there, and the road's gonna be empty, Jonathan was thinking. You'll go back to town, and you'll find George and Greg and Richard sitting in town, you know, drinking a Coke out there at P&S Foods. Greg is a fuckup, he'll never do it. He'll never go through with it. You'll see.

Then, up ahead, walking by side of the road ...

Shit! Jonathan thought. He jammed the brakes, slid to a stop. Richard jumped in, then Greg.

"Did you all just do what I think you all did?" asked Jonathan.

"Yeah, man, come on, let's go!" said Greg. "Let's get out of here."

Jonathan floored it. Richard looked really scared, just scared, no emotion to it at all. His eyes were huge. He hung his head. Greg, by the door, was hyper. Paranoid and real hyper.

"Man, did you really kill this dude?" asked Jonathan. "I mean, is he dead? Is he layin' out there in the fucking field dying, you know, dead?"

"Yeah, man," rasped Greg, "Shut up! Just keep on driving!"

"Shot him three times, man," said Richard. "He's dead."

"Fuuu-uuck," said Jonathan, low and long, in two syllables. "Fuuu-uuuck."

Charles "Chuck" Pinto first saw Midlothian in the spring of 1986. It was a Saturday, and he and his wife had packed a bag and driven 250 miles north from Live Oak, bound for the town that was courting him for a job as city manager.

Though Pinto craved the challenge of a new town, he was first of all a family man, and he knew well the heart-pull of uprooting. As a city manager, he'd be working late, attending countless meetings. The entire community and its entire portfolio of problems and pissing matches would be his responsibility. In short, taking a job in Midlothian meant that he, his wife, and his two kids would have to live there.

Pinto, who was thirty-six at the time, probably realized that he had the advantage on this job transaction. Midlothian was badly in need of a city manager, and he was known as a dynamo. A former Houston Police Department traffic-accident investigator and small-town police chief, Pinto had turned around the city of Live Oak, his first assignment, in just six and a half years. An air force veteran with a bachelor's degree in criminal justice and a master's in public administration, the lean, clean, hardworking Pinto typified a trend in city managers in recent years, a move away from engineers or native sons toward law-and-order, can-do professionals.

The citizens of Midlothian knew that they, too, could have prosperity if they planned for it. They had watched over the years as one by one their neighbors to the north had been transformed magically from sleepy farm towns into bustling suburbs. In the last ten years, Midlothian had already become a bit of a bedroom community, and the numbers were ripe for exploitation. Between 1970 and 1986, the city population had more than doubled, as workers from Dallas sought housing within a commutable distance. By the late eighties, only 10 percent of Midlothian's residents were working at the steel and concrete plants that for years had employed most of the residents in the area. Median family income had risen from about $23,000 in 1980 to $34,000 in 1985. And although Midlothian, in 1986, encompassed only thirteen square miles, surrounding it were twenty-two square miles of land that could be legally annexed.

As always, Pinto had done his homework. Midlothian, he could see, had excellent prospects. The city had recently begun turning a profit with its electrical franchise, selling electricity to its neighbors. It had begun work on a new reservoir, a water-processing plant, and a million-gallon storage tank. The U.S. government had just awarded

Midlothian and neighboring Waxahachie a grant to plan a commercial airport. It had also declared the town and some surrounding areas an international free-trade zone, creating the opportunity for the high-profit deferred-duty sale of imported products.

And so it was that Chuck Pinto and his wife pulled their Olds Cutlass into Midlothian after a five-hour drive on that rainy Saturday afternoon, intending to look around, check the shopping, eat dinner, and stay overnight.

Pinto was shocked. Was this the place he had researched? No curbs, gutters, or street signs. No hotel, no shopping center, nowhere to stay overnight. No drainage. Helter-skelter development. "In a town facing high growth and development," Pinto said, "there's always a lot of controversy. Here, I knew I'd be in for it."

The Pintos drove around town for two hours. Then they drove all the way back home.

But Midlothian kept after Chuck Pinto, and he returned for interviews. He met the people, toured the schools. He changed his mind.

"I guess when you compare values," Pinto said, "you always compare yourself. I'm from a modern but yet very conservative attitude. That's what I saw. A lot of people with good values. There were good church values, first. Now that doesn't mean a hill of beans to me, because a lot of people can go to church, and it doesn't mean a thing. But what I saw was people who had religious values about them whether they were in church or not. I saw it in practice. I saw the stability in the community."

So Pinto took the job and moved his family, and beginning in July 1986, he began the task of modernizing Midlothian.

He computerized and organized, helped put the city in the black for the first time in years. He urged the city to annex four square miles of land. He brought in paid firefighters, folded the ambulance service into the fire department, initiated a policy of crosstraining whereby a firefighter was also a paramedic and a building inspector. Road signs were erected, community services were put in place, the police force was overhauled and retrained, and a new police chief, a twenty-year man from Dallas, was hired.

In addition, a "comprehensive plan" was commissioned—at a cost of $160,000, more than five times the average amount spent on similar small-city plans. The plan specified that future development should take into account "that the character of Midlothian is primarily that of a small town, and that community facilities should provide a sense of community identity."

And perhaps most important, Pinto was a key player in Ellis County's bid to land the U.S. Department of Energy's Superconducting Super Collider, a $4.5 billion energy project. Pinto knew that if the county was chosen as the site, it would instantly become the energy capital of the world. The project, Pinto knew, would bring higher standards of education, sophistication, permanent stability, and economic boom. The proposed location for the facility was next door to Midlothian.

So times and hopes were high in the city. Then one morning in early 1987, Pinto pulled into a gas station and convenience mart near city hall.

"I watched some kids trading drugs and money," said Pinto. "You could see it was routine. We had received some information from various sources that we were a distribution point for drugs, in that a lot of the trucks come through here. I was sitting here thinking, 'Are we furnishing the world with drugs?'"

As Pinto saw it, before anything could be done, officials had to learn the extent of the drug traffic in town. He went to the city council, asked for funds for a "covert" drug operation. As Pinto said, "You come into a town like this and you tell them, 'I'd like to have some money to buy some drugs.' Well, you've got to break people into that slowly."

In the end, however, there was little fuss over the proposal. Though Pinto said the council members weren't told "exactly what we were doing," they were given the general idea. There was a drug problem in town, and Pinto knew something they could do about it.

In a community like Midlothian, *drug problem* means any drugs at all. Two years into Nancy Reagan's Just Say No program, Midlothian was highly aware of drugs and their toll on the nation. With nearly every home wired for cable TV, even a rural town like Midlothian was linked by satellite to every fashion and fad, every event, attitude, and phobia experienced by the collective national mind. The citizens and leaders of Midlothian knew well about the war on drugs, and they knew that *everyone* had to fight. They appropriated $20,000.

Surely another reason the council went along was the recent installment of Roy Vaughn as chief of police. Vaughn, 53, a big man with a full head of white hair, had spent twenty-two years on the Dallas police force and had been the assistant coordinator of Dallas's Organized Crime Unit. Equally important to the townspeople was the fact that Vaughn was one of the family, a twenty-year resident of Midlothian. He was a member of the chamber of commerce and had put five kids through the school system. When he retired from the Dallas force in 1980, he had opened Midlothian Glass and Mirror.

In January 1987, Vaughn beat out forty-one other applicants to become chief. "I think I missed the police work," he said.

To help with the narcotics investigation, Vaughn brought in Billy Fowler. Short and dark, with a deeply creased face, Fowler was given the rank of lieutenant in the twelve-man, nine-car Midlothian force. Like Vaughn, Fowler had spent more than twenty years with the Dallas police force. For a time, he'd worked exclusively in narcotics, usually as a "control agent," the in-house contact of the man undercover.

For their operation, Vaughn and Fowler borrowed police officers from nearby Cedar Hill. Between May and August of 1987, the undercover agents bought marijuana, cocaine, and amphetamines in small but felonious quantities from sources around town. By August, when the operation ended, seventeen adults had been arrested on twenty-eight felony counts.

"Through this investigation," said Vaughn, "we determined we had a problem in the high school. We had good information. I can truthfully say that in May we arrested two seventeen-year-olds for sale of methamphetamine. Neither of them were students, but during the investigations we readily found places where high school kids were buying and using marijuana on the premises. We determined we had a problem in the high school."

"We weren't just picking on Midlothian," said Pinto. "We had a lot of kids coming over here from other areas. Some of the other towns around here had been doing some pretty good drug enforcement, and there was a void in Midlothian. If I put a dead-bolt lock on my door, and you leave yours open, and somebody wants to do a burglary, they're going into your place. Well, other towns were throwing some drug dead bolts up, and we had our door open.

"So we just closed the door. We said, 'We need to get to that younger group.' And the way to get into that younger group was to get somebody that fit into the high school age."

George William Raffield never knew his father, who left the family before George was born. When he was seven months old, his mother, Shirley, who worked in a nursing home, married Don Moore, a machinist. It was Moore's second marriage as well, and among the seven children in the newly combined household was another George, so the baby was called Tiger.

Tiger was one of those boys who declare one day early in life that they want to be policemen, and he never wavered from that goal. By his sophomore year at Mesquite High, southwest of Dallas, George joined the Police Explorers, and by his senior year, he'd risen to captain.

A straight kid who never smoked or drank, Tiger had one vice: cinnamon rolls. The habit produced a small spare tire around his midsection of his five-foot-five-inch frame—and not a little teasing from his sisters, Sheryl and Sherrie. He was extremely close to the girls, his natural sisters, especially Sheryl. There were only thirteen months between Tiger and Sheryl; they were best friends. Tiger introduced Sheryl to David, the boy she would marry. Sheryl, in turn, coached Tiger before his first kiss. It was Tiger's freshman year, the Valentine's dance.

Sheryl and David and George and Dolly had doubled, Sheryl remembered. "Dolly was sitting next to me, and she said, 'Is your brother gonna kiss me?' and I said, 'I don't know.' So I asked him. I said, 'Tiger, are you gonna kiss Dolly?' He says, "Well, I don't know. How should I do it?' and I said, 'Just go up to her and lay one on her!' And that's just what he did."

George's accounting teacher at Mesquite remembered that the 1985 graduate "was not the typical nerd. George was a well-rounded kid. He could horse around, but he could read people. If I said, 'Okay, now, y'all get busy,' he would go around and tell everyone to get busy. He wanted to clean up the world."

After graduation, George continued on at Minyard's Food Stores, where he had worked since he was fifteen, giving all but thirty-five dollars of his weekly paycheck to his mother. He also enrolled at Tarrant County Junior College and took an eleven-week course to earn his basic police certificate. Though busy with work and studies, George also found time to join the reserve police force in Red Oak, the town where his family had recently moved, five miles northeast of Midlothian. As a reserve officer, he wore a uniform and carried handcuffs, and almost every Friday night he'd patrol Red Oak High School activities. Often, George would ride in patrol cars with Red Oak officers, putting in three or four times the required sixteen hours a month of service, working Christmas and Thanksgiving so the regulars could stay home.

When George graduated, he received his police certificate and his first handgun, a nickel-plated, wood-handled Smith & Wesson .357 Magnum, purchased for about $300 at the police-supply store in Grand Prairie. "He was nineteen," said Shirley Moore. "He wasn't old enough to buy the gun or the bullets to go in it. We had to buy it for him. He always carried that gun. I used to get so frustrated because he put it in his back waistband when we'd go into a big shopping center. And I'd say, 'Tiger, do you always have to carry that?' and he'd say, 'Yes, Mother, we always have to carry it.'"

In September of 1986, George got his first real job, with the Wilmer police force. Not long after he started, George wrecked two patrol cars while chasing speeders. "He didn't do anything wrong," said Wilmer police chief Preston Parks. "He just had some bad luck." Nevertheless, George was let go after three months. Sergeant Michael Pigg, the officer who had trained George, said he was fired for "failure to meet minimum standards for probation ... for violating policy involving the operation of patrol cars."

"George was a damn good man," said Pigg. "He would have made a fine officer. He just couldn't handle the cars."

Returning to Red Oak, George began working part-time as a police dispatcher. Then, in June of 1987, Roy Vaughn called. Vaughn had heard about the enthusiastic young cop who was looking for a job. He told George he had an assignment that was perfect for him. He couldn't discuss the details over the phone.

"I looked for several candidates," said Vaughn, "and George kind of fit the role for what I was looking for. He was an impressive-type kid. He was an average-type Joe. Good, clean-cut disposal. Followed instruction well. I was looking for someone I could put out there and know he could do the job. Some guys go out there, they get too close to the people they're working against. They can go bad. We knew that wouldn't happen to George."

In August, George was sent for about a month of training with the Dallas Police Department's narcotics unit. They "took him under their wing, showed him the dos and the don'ts," Vaughn said.

According to his mother, George participated in several drug raids in Dallas. "One night he came home and said he'd just been out on this bust, and he said he was so tired of counting money. He said that's all he'd done, was count money. He said, 'Mother, you wouldn't believe the drugs and the money.'"

Following the training, George worked closely with Billy Fowler. First, they "laid down his cover." For the purpose of the investigation, George William Raffield would be known to all as William George Moore, though he'd still go by George, so he'd remember to answer to his name.

George Moore's story was that he had come from Temple, Texas, was living with an uncle in Midlothian and was buying the drugs to resell in Temple, where he had a girlfriend he visited on weekends.

One day in late July, George and Fowler drove to Temple. "We wanted him to be well acquainted with the town," said Fowler, "in case he ran into somebody at the school who might ask him where the Dairy Queen is."

George and Fowler also went over to Temple High School. With the help of the principal and a guidance counselor, William George Moore was entered into the computer system, given a Temple address, vaccine records, and a transcript of courses from grades one through eleven. George Moore's grades were made a little lower than average. "We didn't want to have him working eight hours on the street and then going home and busting his ass doing a bunch of homework," said Fowler.

With his cover established and his mustache shaved, George was enrolled in Midlothian High as a twelfth grader. None of the school's officials was told of the existence of an undercover officer in the school.

Still, George had much to learn. "All this stuff was really new to him," said Fowler. "He'd never been around drugs at all. He didn't smoke cigarettes. He didn't even drink. We asked him, if he was forced to, could he drink a can of beer. He said he probably could if he tried, but he never had.

"We told him, 'If you're buying weed, you're probably going to run into a situation where you're gonna at least have to simulate smoking it.' We showed him how to pinch it off and actually not get any of the smoke but to still act like you do. We told him, 'Number one, go over there and don't rush into it.' We really didn't care if he didn't make any buys for the first four or five or six weeks. We told him to try and sort the kids out in his mind, you know, who were the dopers, who were the ropers, who were the preppies. We told him not to ever buy any drugs in school, never to be in possession of any drugs in school. Not to get in trouble in school. To maintain a rapport with the teachers. Not to be a problem student. To call us every night. To call us before and after a buy. To be in school every day or, if he wasn't gonna be in school, to let us know. We'd check the school parking lot two or three times a day to see if his truck was there. We knew that playing hooky would be part of the game, but we told him, 'Just let us know first, 'cause if you're not there in school, we don't know where you are.'"

George Moore registered for English, typing, math, computer science, and health at Midlothian High. When the first fall-semester grades came out, the undercover agent was on the honor roll.

In English, he wrote an essay about horse racing and chose to write a book report about *The Sword in the Stone*. His handwriting, according to his teacher, Harriette Fowler, was a lovely cursive, and he was "just a little more advanced than most of the kids as far as vocabulary and writing skills."

In health class, George's handwriting was sloppy, and he often left the bottom half of the test papers unfinished. "The only thing he'd say was, you know, 'It's Friday! We're gonna party!'" said his teacher, Cathy Britton. "He was no more vague than your normal type of kid."

In typing, George sat himself near the lower-level students. Asked to type a history of himself, he wrote, "My name is George and I am a seventeen-year-old senior. I like to go cruising and partying. ... I think school is boring." In the opinion of George's typing teacher, Barbara Whitham, his was "the work of a very low-level student." On one occasion, however, he made the teacher wonder. While taking a timed test, George typed for a period, then stopped. The clock was still ticking. When the papers were handed in, Whitham saw that George had typed exactly twenty-seven lines, just enough for a D. Every line was perfect.

Students remember George tossing balled-up pieces of paper around the room, helping a classmate cheat on a test, hanging around and watching people. One girl thought George was "laid-back and nice and real quiet ... real intellectual." A boy remembered Friday nights with George. "We'd park our trucks and sit on our tailgates in town and holler at people."

By all accounts, George's first three weeks went smoothly. "He met some guys up there during the first three or four weeks that probably used dope but didn't sell dope," said Fowler. "He liked the guys, they liked him. They'd go out and play flag football, take their four-wheel-drive vehicles and carry him out to the country and ride some mudholes. He was getting paid a good salary, getting all the spending money he needed. He really enjoyed it."

Because there were no movie theaters or teen centers in town, the kids of Middle of the Ocean took their fun where they found it. The video arcade, the bowling alley, and the McDonald's were eleven miles away, in Waxahachie; the mall was even farther away, in Duncanville; the liquor store was farther still, in South Dallas.

Most of the Midlothian kids didn't have much money anyway. Their parents worked blue-collar jobs; their allowances were pretty much slim, five or ten dollars a week. The major form of entertainment in Midlothian was cruising. An offshoot of cruising was "rafting." The kids would park their cars and pickups close together, side by side, and put the windows down, and they'd all tune their radios simultaneously to Z-ROCK, and they'd yell back and forth between cars.

That was about it in Midlothian, besides sex and drugs.

By the dopers' own rough estimate, about 10 percent of the 750 students at the high school smoked dope on occasion. Half of those considered themselves "true dopers," kids who got high, according to one of them, "at least once a day, several times a day if we can."

To tell the truth, the dopers of Midlothian couldn't afford to take drugs in massive quantities, but they did well in the area of variety. Marijuana and hashish. Cocaine, both powder and crack. LSD of varying kinds and strengths. PCP and crank, a powdered amphetamine.

Since Midlothian's summer offensive against drugs, the only place to score, according to the dopers, was out of town, either on Polk Street in Dallas or in neighboring towns and cities. Because of this, the dopers operated in a spirit of cooperation and trust that mirrored the small-town ways of their parents. If someone was going to Dallas to make a buy, he would buy for a few others as well. It made sense: less money was wasted on gas; not everyone had a car; and some kids weren't yet old enough to drive. Though their parents would never have understood this, drugs were a matter of friendship to the dopers of Midlothian High, a common denominator that crossed differences in age and class and status. Drugs were something to share, something to gather over, something to do in the Middle of the Ocean.

After three weeks at school, George began spending less time with the "fun" kids and more time with the dopers. One of his new friends was Greg Knighten.

Since Greg couldn't drive and had pretty much lost his regular ride now that Jonathan and Richard were hanging around together all the time, George came in handy. He began picking Greg up for school and taking him home afterward. And as it would develop, George would buy many bags of dope with Greg's help.

According to Fowler, George's first opportunity to make a buy came on Thursday, September 18. When school was over, George met a doper friend in the parking lot, at the red truck.

The doper asked if George had seen a friend of theirs.

"No, but his truck's still over there," said George.

The doper walked to the other truck, waited for the kid, spoke to him, and returned. "He's gonna bring me some weed tomorrow," he told George.

"And here, George seized the opportunity," said Fowler. "He told the doper to get him a twenty-five-dollar bag."

The next day in school, Fowler said, the doper asked George for the money. Later that day, during a pep rally in the cafeteria, George watched money change hands. "He said this kid had a pad and a pencil out and two or three kids were standing in line. He was taking their orders, taking their money. Right in the cafeteria."

George called Fowler and told him that the deal would go down before the football game. Fowler said he'd meet George at the game. "We had a prearranged signal that he was to give me in the crowd. I told him that when we made eye contact, if he had scored, just to run his hand through his hair, which he did.

"I went into the restroom, and he came into the restroom, and he told me he had the dope in his truck, locked in his glove compartment. I told him I was gonna leave at half time and for him to leave as soon after that as he could, because he was supposed to be going to Temple to see his girlfriend."

After an interval, George left the game and drove out in the country to Fowler's house, looping around, making sure he wasn't being followed. As would become standard procedure, Fowler left his electric garage door open, and George pulled in silently and shut the door. George surrendered the drugs, then sat and drank a Coke and related the details of the buy.

As weeks passed, this late-night scene at Fowler's place would become more regular. "George would give Knighten money and say, 'Well, when you score, will you get me two quarters?'—or three, or whatever he was buying." Fowler said. "So they'd go to Dallas, and George would remain in his truck. That's the way the cases would be made on Knighten. We in turn were keeping Dallas narcotics informed of where they were scoring.

"George was real proud of what he did. I know one time he brought me either four or six bags that he scored at one time. He'd made two round trips to Dallas the same evening. Boy, he thought he'd really done something."

George was still living with his parents in Red Oak during this time. After coming home from school, he'd eat dinner and go back out. "He'd say, 'Mother, I'm going to make the buy,'" said Shirley Moore.

"He'd never tell me who, but we would discuss what he was going to buy. Sometimes it was marijuana. Then he got on something called crank. I'd heard of crack, but I'd never heard of crank. So he goes in and takes a little sandwich bag out of his drawer, and he says, 'Mom, here's twenty-five dollars' worth.'

"Of course, all that would make me worry, but Tiger used to tell me, he'd say, 'Mother, don't worry; this is high school kids.'"

If you asked people about Greg Knighten, said a former close friend, "they woulda said, 'He's weird, he's nuts, he's a heavy druggie, he's always in trouble, always.' He hated school. He wanted to get the hell out of his parents' house, but he couldn't, 'cause he couldn't get enough money. He thought that life sucked. He said it very often, you know: 'Life sucks.' And he was just waiting until he could get money. That's all he wanted, enough money to get out on his own. That and some friends, some friends to talk to."

Greg Knighten was the adopted son of a Dallas police corporal and his wife, a phys. ed. instructor at a fundamentalist Bible academy. The Knightens, along with Greg and their younger son, had moved to Midlothian two years earlier from Duncanville, a suburban city fifteen miles to the north that had once been a quiet rural town like Midlothian.

Before being assigned to a patrol car in southwest Dallas, Tom Knighten, 44, had worked for many years at the police shooting range, where he met Vaughn. "He was a very good individual, a very helpful individual," Vaughn said. "If you went out to the pistol range, Tom Knighten was the type that if you had problems, he'd go out of his way to help you."

Knighten said that his son, when he was younger, was a quick boy, eager to help his father work on cars, eager to hear police stories, which reminded the young boy of "something just like he'd seen on TV."

"We were a good family, tried to give our sons the right things," said Knighten, who bought the boys, at different times, a swimming pool, a dune buggy, a three-wheel ATV, an off-road motorcycle, and a racing go-cart. "There were good times—lots of them."

According to his father, Greg's problems began in Duncanville. All of a sudden, it seemed, Greg became tired of church. He'd gone to his mother's Bible school since first grade, and now he was insisting on going to a "normal school." He began hanging out with the unsavory kids in town. It seemed to the Knightens that Duncanville was going to the dogs and that Greg was being dragged down with it. It was time to move.

The Knightens found Midlothian. "It was a little town that seemed like the place where I grew up," said Tom Knighten. "We felt like in a nice little town he wouldn't get into much trouble because it just wasn't there."

In Midlothian, Greg became even more distant, and Tom Knighten did not like the look of his son's new friends. Once, Knighten patted down a neighborhood boy for drugs. Later, he questioned teachers about his son's friends, searched his son's room for drug paraphernalia, sent Greg four times for drug tests.

After Greg put a red streak in his hair, the Knightens took him to a psychologist in Dallas.

"We just decided it must be low self-esteem, especially since he was adopted versus our other son being our biological child," Tom Knighten said. "We tried to tell him that being adopted meant he was the chosen one, but to what extent that he heard or believed anything we said, who knows?"

Meanwhile, Greg was having a hard time making friends. Most of the dopers wouldn't go near his house, fearing his father. Many said Greg was a thief. A boy said he stole a camera; a girl said he stole a tape, a hat, and a cross earring; another boy beat him up for stealing a Mötley Crüe cassette.

"He was always screwing somebody around," said one doper. "Like even on a little half-ass deal. He'd go, 'Yeah, I'll get you a dime on Polk Street,' and then he'd come back and give you a nickel and shit, like two joints, and you'd beat his ass for it.

"He wasn't popular. He was kind of a down person, a low person, kind of like a nerd or something. When he hung around us, you know, he was in the way and stuff. He always tried to get us to take him places."

Greg's girl, Jamie Cadenhead, saw him differently. "I know that a lot of people say that he was bad, and he wasn't," she said.

Jamie and Greg planned to get married when they turned seventeen. Then they were going to get an apartment and finish high school. Greg, a talented mechanic, believed he'd have little trouble finding a job. "A lot of people are saying that he didn't care about life," said Jamie. "He did. He made people laugh. When somebody was upset, he'd just get them to feeling better."

Cynthia Fedrick was also fond of Greg. The two had met through her brother, Randy Marcott, another student at Midlothian. Cynthia had married at fifteen and divorced at seventeen. She had two daughters, aged six and four. One lived with the child's father, the other with Cynthia's parents. Cynthia had a bad knee and many worries. "Greg was caring," said Cynthia. "Every time I had a problem, he's been there to talk to."

Though he seemed to have good friends in Jamie and Cynthia, Greg couldn't go see them because he couldn't drive. That's where the new kid, George Moore, came in. Unlike Jonathan Jobe and the others, George seemed willing to take Greg anywhere he wanted to go.

The two boys became fast friends, or so it seemed. Even Greg's parents liked George. When the Knightens had a family dinner for Greg's sixteenth birthday, George was invited to come.

"He just seemed real nice, clean-cut," says Tom Knighten, "and he'd look at you when you talked. That night, we all held hands to say the blessing, and we just felt like he was one of our family. We just felt so pleased that he was there for our son."

On Friday, October 23, the Midlothian Panthers were scheduled to play the Red Oak Hawks. A pep rally was set for that morning, and the late bell would be ringing any minute. The weekend was coming, and lockers were banging, and couples were snatching French kisses, and kids were bombing through the hallways, laughing and high-fiving, walking fast but not running, caught in the spirit of a free period at Middle of the Ocean High.

Richard and Jonathan were at Richard's locker, which was decorated inside with drawings of skulls and pentagrams and things. Down the hall, coming fast, was Greg Knighten.

"Richard! Jonathan! Hey, dudes!"

"Wonder where he wants us to take him now," mumbled Jonathan.

Richard made one of his faces, a real roper face. He spoke in a roper accent, a thick prairie twang. "*Wayyyyy-ellllllllll, Ah jus' don' know, duuuuuuuuuude.*"

Greg was out of breath, hyper, oblivious to the joke. "We pieced together a puzzle, man," he said. "That guy George is a narc. There's got to be something done about it!"

Jonathan stared at Greg a few seconds. Then he said, "What are you talking about?"

"Well, we just pieced it together, believe me. We know this dude is a narc."

Greg ticked off the evidence. The expensive truck. What Jamie's mother had said about a narc at school. The dealers on Polk Street who had been arrested. The police confiscating the stolen stereo from Cynthia.

Jonathan leaned close. He knew that Greg was real smart about putting things together. Usually, if there was anything Greg wanted to do, or wanted to know, he would figure it out. Jonathan also knew Cynthia, and that worried him even more.

Once a doper had ripped off Cynthia for fifty dollars. Greg was friends with this guy, and he wanted Cynthia to know that he wasn't responsible. Greg begged Jonathan to drive him to Cynthia's apartment.

Cynthia was "big, fat, mean, crazy, nuts," said Jonathan. When Greg tried to explain, Cynthia flipped. She pulled down a whole set of shelves; tapes and a radio fell all over the place. She busted the table and busted the chair. She screamed, stomped, kicked stuff around, kicked the wall. Then she grabbed a bottle of bourbon and downed three shots. That's when the boys left.

Now she was pissed again. Some kids would tell the police that Cynthia had grabbed Greg, pushed him against a wall. She had told him to kill George and that if he didn't do it, she'd do it or find someone else to do it.

"And Cynthia said we need to do something about it because George is using us to bust everybody," Greg was telling the other two boys. "She said that when George was done, he's gonna bust me too. Man, that guy has been using us! He's gonna bust me. He's gonna bust Jamie! She's been to Polk Street with me and George! Man. ... Shit. ... That guy came to my birthday party!"

Jonathan looked at Greg. Granted, this was serious, but granted also was the fact that Greg was always getting ready to kick someone's ass, though he rarely ever went through with it.

"So what are you gonna do, kick his ass?" asked Jonathan.

"Yeah, right," said Richard.

"No, man," said Greg. "I'm gonna get a gun."

On Fridays, George's last class was typing. When the bell rang, everyone bolted. George stood a few moments by his desk, waiting for the room to clear. Then he walked toward the teacher's desk. He mumbled something.

"Pardon me?" asked Barbara Whitham. She was a bit shocked. George had rarely spoken in her class.

Now George turned, gestured toward the bulletin board that Whitham had decorated for Halloween. On a black background were orange letters that spelled, DO THESE GHOSTS HAUNT YOU? Surrounding the letters were white construction-paper ghosts. Each ghost was labeled with a different hindrance to good typing: POOR

POSTURE, POOR RHYTHM, and so on. "These ghosts haunt me," George said.

"Which one?" asked Whitham.

"All of them," said George.

George stood, silent. It seemed to Whitham that he wanted to talk, that he had something to say, but he wasn't saying it.

Whitham walked toward him, smiled. "Well, let's not worry about it," she said. "We can start working on those things Monday."

At 6:30 that night, Richard was holding a séance in Greg's bedroom. He had his eyes closed, and his Ouija, Terry's Heart, was on the dresser. Greg and Jonathan stood to either side of him. All three boys pressed their fingertips to the dresser top.

Terry's Heart began to shudder.

Holy shit, thought Jonathan.

Jonathan and Richard had arrived twenty minutes earlier, as Greg had requested. Much to their surprise, Greg actually had a gun. He also had a plan.

It would be a cinch, Greg had said. Who would ever suspect them? George would be dead; the cops wouldn't know anything. And best of all, nobody would go to jail for drugs.

The gun Greg planned to use was one of his father's .38-caliber pistols. Greg had fired it before at the police range. He said that when he took the gun, it had been loaded with fancy bullets. He had removed the fancy ones and replaced them with homemade reloads he had found in the workshop. When they were finished, Greg said, he would put the fancy bullets back, and no one would ever know they'd used it.

Then Greg begged Richard to go with him. For ten minutes he begged, and in the course of that time, Richard's attitude slowly changed from "No way" to "I don't know" to "What could it hurt?" to "Okay, if it means that much to you, dude."

Now, a few minutes later, Terry's Heart was on the dresser. The question lingered in the air: "Is George Moore a narc?"

Terry's Heart shuddered. It moved to the left.

Left meant yes.

Other questions were put. Terry answered.

"Take care of it," it told the boys.

It also had a message for Richard: "Don't do it. Don't go."

A light mist was falling as George's red truck pulled off Farm Road 875 and bounced a quarter mile along a dirt lane through a pasture. George parked facing south. The cement plant glowed in the distance. He engaged the emergency brake, killed the engine, turned the key to auxiliary, and tuned the radio to Z-ROCK. Then all three boys got out of the truck, leaving the doors open so they could hear the music.

They sat on the tailgate, talked about nothing. Everything seemed normal. No allegations were mentioned. Nothing was said about narcs. After a while, one of the boys said, "George, would ya go and turn that music up some?"

George hopped down, turned, and started toward the driver's door, with one of his hands in the pocket of his navy-blue jacket.

The first shot hit George square in the back of the head. As he fell, the second shot grazed the side of his head. The third shot missed. George was dead by the time he hit the ground.

"Fuuu-uuck," said Jonathan, low and long. "Fuuu-uuuck."

At about 7:45 p.m., Jonathan saw what he had hoped he wouldn't see, Richard and Greg walking along Farm Road 875. He stopped his truck, and the boys tumbled in.

"Get the hell over to Cynthia's," said Greg. "We got his wallet, man."

"Fuck, man," said Jonathan. "I want my fucking gas money and then you get the hell out of here."

"Man, you got to take me to Jamie's," said Greg. "Please, man."

On the way to Cynthia's apartment, Greg opened George's wallet, divided up the eighteen dollars he found inside. Had the boys checked the front pocket of George's blue jeans, they would have found $50.52. They would not, however, have found his gun. George's nickel-plated .357 Magnum was not on him. Unlike the undercover cops on 21 Jump Street, his favorite TV show, George was not allowed to carry a weapon on assignment. George's gun, along with his real wallet, was back in his apartment. Twenty-two days earlier, two weeks after his twenty-first birthday, George had moved out of his mother's house for the first time. He shared his new place with his fiancée. They were to be married in April.

When the boys arrived at Cynthia's apartment, the usual crowd was partying, some of them students, some not. According to Cynthia, "Greg started to tell me about having his daddy's gun, and how he'd switched from the fancy bullets to regular bullets. That's when I told him to shut up."

Nevertheless, Cynthia took the wallet from the boys, and she went into the bedroom, where she burned George Moore's driver's license over an ashtray. Why she did this is not clear. Later, the police would find the wallet intact in her trash.

Next, at Greg's insistence, the boys drove to Jamie's. They said little en route. When they pulled up, Greg stepped out of the truck, and Jamie came running out of the house. They hugged. Greg cried.

"It's all okay now," he told her.

In his bedroom, Jonathan had his collection of G.I. Joe dolls and samurai swords, and like many of the kids in Midlothian, he also had his own phone, complete with call waiting and conference call. When he and Richard returned from Jamie's, Richard phoned Gina, his girlfriend, and told her what had happened.

Gina said she and others had heard Greg talking about his plan at school, had heard him saying, "He's a narc, man. I'm gonna kill his ass." Other kids had heard about the events from the partyers at Cynthia's. Tales of the séance and the shooting were buzzing in bedrooms all over town.

Richard and Jonathan couldn't sleep. Jonathan was pretty freaked out, but he knew he hadn't done anything, and he knew his parents would believe him. Unlike his two friends, he'd never been in any trouble. The very worst thing he'd ever done in his life was start a fire in a field.

Richard, on the other hand, was scared out of his mind. He was there. He'd seen George dead. It wasn't the first time he'd been present during a felony. Four months earlier, in June, Richard had witnessed the bludgeoning of a sixteen-year-old boy. Frank Ross, a nineteen-year-old, was charged with the attack, which took place in a trailer on a farm owned by Richard's grandparents. Richard's father, a hairdresser and heavy-equipment operator, and his mother, a waitress, lived in the main house of the farm. Richard, who lived alone in the trailer, was the only eyewitness. The victim survived, though he suffered six skull fractures and was comatose for nine days.

Richard and Jonathan talked most of the night in Jonathan's room. They didn't know what to do. They discussed hiding out in Arizona. Richard knew someone there who might help, the son of a highway patrolman who lived in Williams. They decided to call him in the morning.

Meanwhile, Billy Fowler was getting worried. George always checked in at ten or eleven in the evening. Fowler called Vaughn.

"It was the middle of the night," Vaughn said. "We came down here to the office and started making calls and checking places. Sometimes, for an undercover officer to disappear for a short period of time, you know that's normal. Billy had talked to him some, ten minutes to seven. George said he was going out to meet some people and just piddle around. There wasn't any planned drug buy, so we weren't overly concerned, but we were concerned. Our city limits is cut up. We got much rural area. I felt, and there was no doubt in my mind, well—I called the Texas Rangers prior to ever finding the body."

At 6:00 a.m., Vaughn called George's mother and told her George was missing. George's stepdad and brother-in-law went hunting for him in their truck. Meanwhile, hundreds of police officers, state and local, on duty and off, joined the search for their missing colleague. Horses, pickups, and four-wheel drives swarmed through the tiny town and the surrounding prairies. Once the cloud cover lifted, helicopters flew concentric circles around Midlothian.

At home, Shirley Moore and her daughters monitored the search with a police scanner her eldest stepson had purchased that morning as soon as the stores opened.

"I was going crazy," she said. "I knew Tiger was dead. I just wanted them to find his body. I knew as soon as the call came, 'cause he was not the type not to check in. He was too dependable.

"I knew his cover had been blown. Right before he moved into his apartment, he told me he had gotten ripped off on a deal, and the chief had told him to go back and stand up, either get his money or his stuff, and what happened was he ended up having an altercation with one kid in a parking lot of a drugstore. That day he told me, he says, 'Mother, the kid hit me, but I couldn't hit him back. Mother, I couldn't hit him. He's only seventeen, and I'm a police officer. I couldn't hit him 'cause he's a minor.' He said the kid accused him of being a narc, and the kid said, 'My dad thinks you're a narc too.'

"And that was the last time I saw him, standing right here. And I said to him, 'Get out. Your cover is blown. Get out of it, or you're gonna be dead.' And he said, 'Oh, Mother, I'm gonna be all right.' And I said, 'No. You tell them. You get out of it.'"

At about 4:00 p.m. on October 24, Shirley Moore heard the message on the scanner. "Victim and vehicle found," a voice said. "Search discontinued. Notify family." A few minutes later, on television, she saw Tiger, lying face down in the field. A few minutes after that, she got word from the police.

An hour later, at about 5:00 p.m., Jonathan, Richard, and Gina pulled up to Richard's house. They'd spent the day at a flea market in Waxahachie. They'd walked around awhile, and then Richard decided he wanted to buy Gina a silver necklace. It was only two nights before that he'd kissed her for the first time; they'd decided to go steady. Richard didn't have enough money to buy the necklace, so he and Jonathan pooled what was left of George's. Gina kicked in what she had, fifty cents.

Now, as Jonathan set the emergency brake and reached to open the door of his truck, a van pulled up across the street. A man stuck his head out of the window and yelled.

"Hey, come here, man, we want to talk to you."

Jonathan, Richard, and Gina exchanged looks. They stepped slowly out of the truck.

Suddenly, there were police cars everywhere. Thirty, maybe more. They came from the left, the right, straight ahead. Cops jumped out, their hands on their guns.

Fuck, man, thought Jonathan. *We're dead. We're gone. Right now, man, this is the end of everything.*

Then he thought, *This is like* Miami Vice!

In late January, after the murder, Chief Vaughn leaned back in a chair in his smoky office. Across the desk was Lieutenant Fowler. Chuck Pinto was in the doorway; he'd come by to talk about the porn busts at two video stores in town.

"The stereo was taken in a burglary," said the chief. "It was an expensive stereo. It was a rented stereo. In a sense, it was a kind of a judgment call. We didn't think any way in the world that it would be connected with George. In all honesty, we searched our souls and everything else. Realistically, hell, if we had to go back and do it again, no, we wouldn't have done it. But that's what happened."

"The whole thing was so unbelievable," said Fowler, and Pinto and Vaughn shook their heads in agreement. "If you were dealing with a bunch of Jamaicans or Puerto Ricans or some hard dudes like that, you might have thought ... But here, to think that some kid from Midlothian would shoot someone, well, how can you even think that?"

"Yeah," said Pinto. "I mean, you might think that if they thought George was a narc—and there was never any indication that he was compromised, believe me—you'd think they woulda whupped his ass, something like that."

Vaughn creaked forward in his big wooden chair and leaned his forearms across the desk. He looked at Pinto and Fowler, and he sighed, and then he searched for the right words. "Quite honestly ... Had we ... You don't think ...Realistically .... Oh, hell." He shook his head. "You can sit back and try and reason all day long, and you never come up with a solution. What I can't figure out is why. You know, why?"

As of this writing, Richard Goeglein, 17, is being held in lieu of bond at the Ellis County jail, indicted on a charge of capital murder, which carries a possible sentence of death by injection. Greg Knighten and Jonathan Jobe, now both sixteen, have been declared adults for trial and have also been indicted on charges of capital murder. As minors, Knighten and Jobe are exempt from the death penalty. Conviction, however, carries a mandatory life sentence. Knighten, whose lawyer has told reporters that his client did not fire the fatal shots, is in the county jail. Jobe is free on a $50,000 bond and is making good grades at Midlothian High.

Cynthia Fedrick, 23, has been indicted on charges of criminal solicitation for capital murder and conspiracy to commit capital murder; both crimes are first-degree felonies. She too is in the county jail, facing penalties of five years to life.

George Moore was buried in his Midlothian P.D. uniform with full police honors and a twenty-one-gun salute. More than 570 officers attended his funeral, and hundreds of townsfolk lined the streets of Waxahachie to see his half-mile-long procession. Five days after his death, he was inducted into the American Police Hall of Fame, in Northport, Florida. A memorial scholarship has been funded in George's name to be awarded each year to a student participating in Midlothian High's Just Say No program.

Ellis County, Texas, with participation from the city of Midlothian, is one of six finalists in the bidding on the U.S. Department of Energy's Superconducting Super Collider. The winner will be announced soon.

RAISED
IN
CAPTIVITY

Gary Fannon lost the best years of his life to a trumped-up arrest, a crooked cop, and draconian drug-sentencing laws. The decade he spent in prison taught him lessons no man should ever have to learn. A campaign spearheaded by *Rolling Stone* magazine and the author help set him free.

He rode out to quarantine on a bus full of stinking guys, all of them under twenty-one, convicted as adults of felony crimes. He was going to Riverside to be processed, three hours away, in Ionia, Michigan. The town had four prisons. They pronounced it *I-own-ya.*

Gary Wayne Fannon Jr. pressed his nose to the vent by the window, seeking fresher air. He wanted to scream, to cry, to smash his head through the glass. The state of Michigan owned him now. He'd drawn the mandatory penalty for his crime: life in prison without parole. It was a death sentence, really—a long, slow death by natural causes.

He stepped off the bus, his wrists shackled to a belt around his waist, his legs chained together at the ankles. He shuffled forward in a single-file line, through a door marked Intake. They removed his shackles, locked the heavy gate behind him. They gave him his number, 189196. He bent over, spread his cheeks, and coughed. He got his blues. The shirts were too big; the pants were too small. The underwear was made by convicts in a factory for twenty-eight cents a day. Since it was summer—August 20, 1987, to be exact, his nineteenth birthday—they were giving out rubber flip-flops. He reached down into a huge laundry cart, held his breath against the smell. The rubber was worn, impressed with the toe prints of previous owners. *Fuck it*, thought Gary. *Happy birthday to me.*

One week, one month, two months, three. An eight-by-ten-foot cell, twenty-three hours a day. No TV, no radio, no roommate. If you needed to piss, you used a plastic bottle. If you needed to do more, you had to bang on the door and wait for the guard. Sometimes the guard wouldn't come, and you'd have to use your trash can. Then you'd tie up the plastic liner bag and throw it out the window, into the courtyard.

The guards at the Riverside Correctional Facility liked Gary. He was polite and well-mannered. He was White, as were most of the guards. He seemed like a regular kid. How he had gotten here, how he had ended up with a life sentence—Gary wondered about that himself. Before all this happened, he had lived with his mom and little brother in an apartment complex in Westland, a blue-collar suburb northwest of Detroit. He played guitar, smoked pot, paid $120 a month on his black Mercury LN7, was a regular at the midnight screening of *The Rocky Horror Picture Show*. He graduated from high school by the skin of his teeth. He'd been in trouble with the law once: nabbed at age thirteen for shoplifting a pack of batteries. The cops never found the other item he'd taken, secreted in his coat pocket, a small ceramic statue of a blond guy in a striped prison suit, a ball and chain affixed to his ankle. Now it seemed like an episode of *Tales From the Crypt*, some eerie prophecy fulfilled.

Why me, oh Lord? Gary asked this many times. He made a list of everything he'd done wrong in his life, looking for a reason he was being punished like this now. When he was seven, he had broken a pinball machine in a bar his father had taken him to. When he was thirteen, he had smashed a window in the front door of an apartment complex. The manager had denied his mother an application; he had a policy against renting to divorcees with kids. When he was twelve, Gary fell in with a bad crowd. They jimmied apartment doors, stole spare change and radios, rearranged furniture. Later they stole car stereos and radar detectors. And there were the little things. Like the time he broke that girl's virginity and then called her a blood witch. The time he hit his kid brother for squealing. The time he raised his fist to his mom, a selfless woman who slept on the sofa in the living room.

Because the guards liked Gary, they gave him the job of cleaning the courtyard. He didn't get paid, but he did get to go outside by himself for an hour. He'd rake the shit bags into a pile and carry them to the dumpster. Then he'd mow the grass. At least it was something to do.

One day he was in his cell and there was nothing to do, he was going insane. He'd written all the letters he could, his hand was numb and there was nothing to do, he was going insane. He'd read as many books as he could, his eyes were killing him. There was nothing to do and the window was open and the sun was shining. He wanted to be outside. He was going insane.

A fly buzzed into his cell. It landed on the windowsill, on the bed, on the desk. Gary watched it.

The fly rubbed its legs together. It flitted around nervously. Gary inched toward it. Closer. Closer. He tried to quiet his body and his brain, to make himself still like deep water, like Caine on *Kung Fu.*

He snapped out his arm and caught the fly in his hand. He put it in a large Doritos bag, purchased in the prison store, contents devoured, bag kept folded on the shelf. He watched the fly buzz around inside the Doritos bag. Time passed.

A bee flew into the cell. Gary watched it. He concentrated, trying to send the bee a telepathic message. *Come to me. Come to me.* The bee settled on the back of his hand. He cupped it in his palm, put it in the Doritos bag; the bee on one end, sectioned off with a pencil, and then the fly, and then a book to seal the opening, all of it on top of the desk.

Gary watched the bee. He watched the fly. Every once in a while, he'd remove the pencil, open up the sections, make them meet so they would fight. But they wouldn't. They just buzzed and walked around.

Time passed. A wasp flew into the cell. The shit bags in the courtyard were like magnets for all these bugs. It was a regular insect zoo. Gary stalked the wasp across the room, caught it in a Styrofoam cup. He put it in the Doritos bag.

He watched some more. He set up fights between the wasp and the fly, the wasp and the bee. The bee and the fly wouldn't fight, but the wasp, he would fight anybody. Gary took turns pitting the wasp against the fly and the wasp against the bee. That was the best match, the wasp against the bee. Lots of buzzing and stinging. Just hours of amusement, you know.

In the end, the fly got crushed. The bee suffocated. The wasp drowned in the Styrofoam cup.

By then it was time for chow.

December 10, 1986. One year earlier ...

Gary sat at the wheel of his Mercury LN7, listening to Pink Floyd's *Dark Side of the Moon*, using the rearview mirror to study a new zit budding on his chin. He was parked behind another place called Riverside, this one a roller rink, waiting to meet a guy named Kurt Johnston, a friend of his buddy Lance's.

Gary and Lance had been hanging out for about a year. Lance had a beer belly and wore a lightning-bolt earring. Most people thought he was a dipshit, but Gary thought he was funny. He chauffeured Lance around, found him a job and a girlfriend. Lance, in turn, kept Gary's car running. Lance's dad had taught him auto mechanics. He was a cop. He didn't like Lance's friends, his hours, his behavior, his attitude, his foul mouth, his pot smoking. Lance lived in the basement, kept a footlocker full of weapons. He had baseball bats with screws stuck in them, brass knuckles, several guns. Lance and his dad fought so much that his dad had recently kicked him out. Gary's mom was letting him stay at their place.

The beginning of Lance and Gary's friendship corresponded roughly with Gary's entry into the pot business. Gary started out selling loose joints during his junior year, later moved into grams and quarter ounces. Occasionally, he sold mescaline or acid. His buyers were students on school grounds at lunchtime. Much of the stuff was consumed on the spot.

Looking back, Gary thinks the reason he started dealing was his new girlfriend. Kathy was a year older, more experienced, a twelfth grader. Kathy liked smoking pot before sex, which was fine with Gary, but it started getting a little expensive. Gary had worked since he was thirteen—busing tables at Chuck E. Cheese, washing dishes at the upscale surf-and-turf roadhouse where his mom waitressed. Wouldn't it be cheaper, Gary proposed, if they bought a quarter ounce of pot and sold joints for a dollar apiece? With the profit, they could smoke for free.

Making Kathy happy was Gary's number one priority. She'd had a shitty life. She didn't know her dad. Her mom worked in a box factory, spent her off-hours sniffing glue. Gary had this thing about taking care of people—running errands, driving them places, lending support. You might say that Gary was searching constantly for love and assurance, trying to be the kind of father figure he had never had.

Gary Sr. was a Tennessee native, an early-1960s greaser who combed his hair into a waterfall. Gary's mom, Linda, the fourth of fourteen children in a loving Catholic family, had gotten pregnant by Gary Sr. when she was seventeen. Gary Sr. and Linda were separated when Gary was six and his brother, Robert, was three. For a long time, Gary hated his name. He vowed that someday he would find his father and beat him up, like he remembered him doing to his mom.

When Lance needed a place to stay, Gary, of course, came through. One day, in the fall after graduation, Lance was hanging out with a friend named Bob. They were smoking pot, playing with Lance's .45. Bob picked up the gun, pointed it at his own temple. "Heh-heh, heh-heh, heh-heh," he giggled, and pulled the trigger.

Luckily, the bullet just took out a chunk of Bob's skull, and he eventually recovered. Lance was arrested on a weapons charge. The cops told him that they'd drop the charge in exchange for the names of any drug dealers he knew. Lance gave up Gary. Then Lance moved back home with his father, started acting like he was mad at Gary. Gary didn't understand; he'd done so much for him.

Even so, when Lance called a month later and asked for a favor, Gary was ready and willing. One of his buddies needed some pot. Could Gary help out?

So it was, on the afternoon of December 10, 1986, that a car pulled up behind the Riverside Roller Rink and parked. Gary got out of his car and walked over, slid into the passenger seat. Kurt Johnston was in his thirties, with slicked-back hair and sunglasses on a bleak winter day. He reminded Gary of a character on *Miami Vice*.

This was the second time Gary had met with Johnston. He said he worked at the Ford plant and sold dope to fellow employees. The day before, at their first meeting, Gary had sold Johnston four small bags of pot—five grams in all, less than one-quarter of an ounce— for sixty dollars. Johnston smelled one bag, seemed pleased. Then he asked if Gary could get him some cocaine. Gary said he'd never even done cocaine. Johnston pressed. "A friend of Lance is a friend of mine," Gary declared, giving Johnston a soul handshake and vowing to try.

Now Gary handed Johnston the coke he'd scored, one-eighth of an ounce, $200 worth. Johnston opened the bag, took out a mirror and a bill. He dumped some of the white powder on the mirror, laid out some lines. He snorted, sniff, sniff. Then he handed the mirror to Gary.

Gary took the mirror, the bill. *I don't know,* he thought, a spooky, singsong voice in his head. *I don't kno-ooow.* He'd never done coke before. The way they talked about it on the news, it made you kill your kids, rape your granny, run around naked in the streets. Johnston watched and waited. *I guess this is what happens in a coke deal,* Gary thought. He snorted, sniff, sniff. It hurt his nose at first, but he didn't really feel anything. *What the fuck is this?* he thought. *Why do people do this?*

Then it hit him. BANG! He felt this power surge, like he could pick up the car and throw it over the roller rink. Just that much power. Superpower. He wanted to dance. He wanted to sing. He tried to maintain. "I think I'm gonna go now," he told Johnston.

Gary walked back to his car. When he opened the door, it felt like he was ripping it off the hinges. He cranked Pink Floyd, pulled out of the parking lot, onto the street, squealing the wheels. *Whoa!* he thought. *This is fucking great!* Weed made him sleepy. Alcohol made him sick. Mescaline and acid were okay, though he hated coming down. But coke, whoa! *This is my drug of choice!* he thought. *This makes me fucking whole.*

In a few minutes, the coke began to wear off. Gary wanted more. He made a U-turn, drove back to Detroit. He bought a gram of coke, took it to Kathy's.

They each did some, and then they started fooling around. They did more and more. Gary had never heard a woman scream like that. He had never lasted so long. They stayed up until dawn.

"Everything is set for tomorrow," Gary said into the pay phone one month later, standing on a nasty corner in Detroit. He had lost fifteen pounds, had bags under his eyes. "I just wanted to say, you know, see ya."

"What are you talking about?" asked Kurt Johnston.

"I'm gone, man," said Gary. "I'm taking my girl to Florida."

"Why don't you just wait a couple of days?" asked Johnston. "Let's get this thing done."

Since that afternoon in early December, Gary had supplied Johnston with coke on two more occasions, a half ounce and then an ounce. Then Johnston said he wanted to buy a kilo—thirty-six ounces, 2.2 pounds. The deal was set for January 7. Johnston met Gary and Michael Thompson, the Detroit man who now supplied Gary with pot and coke, in a crummy apartment in Dearborn. Johnston produced $32,000 cash. Gary counted it, all hundreds and twenties and tens. "This is $32,000, all right," Gary announced. He handed it back to Johnston.

"Where's the dope?" asked Johnston.

"We don't have it yet," said Gary.

"Were you planning on getting it?" asked Johnston.

Gary and Thompson left the apartment. They spent all day making phone calls and waiting, trying to get the dope. No luck. The next day, they tried again. Still no luck.

By late afternoon on January 8, Johnston was ballistic. Gary was getting scared. *Maybe this is fucked up, you know?* At first he'd gotten Johnston the drugs as a favor to Lance. Then he'd gotten them as a favor for Johnston. Then he'd gotten them to get free coke. With each deal, he'd skim some coke off the top. Johnston did it; why not he? *I guess this is what happens in a coke deal.* But now, well, things were getting really out of hand. "You guys are a bunch of shit," Johnston bellowed. "Get the hell out!"

Gary drove Thompson back to his house in central Detroit. On the way, they decided to call the supplier one more time. He finally had the stuff. Or most of it, twenty-six ounces. Gary rang Johnston from the pay phone. Johnston agreed to buy the twenty-six ounces for the same price he'd agreed to pay for the thirty-six ounces. The deal was set for the next day. Gary felt his obligations had now been fulfilled. He wasn't getting a cut; he wanted no more part. "Look," he told Johnston from the pay phone, "I'll catch you guys later." He hung up.

Gary took Thompson to the supplier's house, bought an eighth of an ounce for himself and drove to Kathy's. Then the couple went over to see some friends of Kathy's.

The two couples played a snorting game involving dominoes and pencil-thick lines of coke. Around dawn they fell asleep.

At eleven the next morning, Kathy woke Gary. His beeper was going crazy, she said. Gary raised his head off the pillow, tried to focus on the digital readout. Mike Thompson's number. Kurt Johnston's number. Each of them several times. "Fuck them!" he said. He went back to sleep.

He finally rose at 6 p.m. A few hours later, he and Kathy left for Florida, setting out in his LN7 through a snowstorm.

The next afternoon, January 10, one hundred miles from the Florida border, Gary was pulled over for speeding.

After a license check, the cop walked back to the driver's side. "You'd better get out of the car, sir—there's a warrant out for your arrest."

"For what?" asked Gary.

"For delivery of over 650 grams of cocaine," the cop said.

"You sure it's me?"

Gary stood before the judge with his head bowed, trying not to cry. It was August 19, 1987, the day before his nineteenth birthday. Gary was wearing an olive-drab prison jumpsuit. Counting today, he'd been in jail 193 days. A month ago, a jury had found him guilty. Now he was back in court for sentencing.

Gary's handsome face was twisted into a hideous mask of pain and remorse and anticipation. He already knew what was going to happen. It was mandated by state law. But he also knew that some

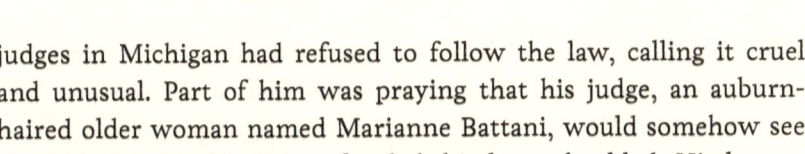

judges in Michigan had refused to follow the law, calling it cruel and unusual. Part of him was praying that his judge, an auburn-haired older woman named Marianne Battani, would somehow see the light too. Gary's vision clouded; his knees buckled. His lawyer caught him with an arm around his waist.

"Have a seat for a minute," said the judge.

Behind Gary, in the front row of the gallery, Linda Fannon was surrounded by family. Her mom sat at her side. "They will not do this to an eighteen-year-old boy," she told Linda.

Neither Linda nor her mom knew about Michigan's "650 drug lifer law." It was passed as a one-paragraph rider to a health-code bill. Very few people knew anything about it, including most of the legislators who had voted for it. The law provided that conviction for delivery of more than 650 grams of cocaine, about 1.4 pounds, carried a mandatory sentence of life in prison without possibility of parole. To be found guilty, you didn't have to deliver any drugs. You didn't have to see any drugs or any money. All you had to do was conspire to possess.

Johnston, of course, was an undercover cop. He lived down the street from Lance's dad. Though Gary was recruited and turned on to coke by the police, and though he was on the road to Florida on January 10 when the twenty-six ounces (723 grams) of coke was delivered, Gary was tried on the same charge at the same trial as Michael Thompson. The jury found the two equally guilty.

Now, at his sentencing, Gary was helped to his feet.

"All right," said the judge. "I have here a stack of letters attesting to how good a person you are and what a nice family you have. And you know what? The court believes all of these things.

"But this court has no discretion whatsoever. It is the sentence of this court that you be committed to the state Department of Corrections for a period of your natural life."

Gary swallowed hard. They will carry me out in a pine box, he thought.

Gary walked into the gym, right on time for band practice.

Basketballs stopped bouncing. The speed bag came to rest. A doo-wop quartet harmonizing in an alcove fell silent. There must have been forty or fifty Black guys in there, every eyeball on him. "Here come the snitch!" somebody hollered. A chorus erupted. "Cheese eater!" "Rat!" "Bitch!"

Gary froze in the doorway, set his feet in a martial-arts T stance. He took a deep breath. He roared: "COME AND GET ME, MOTHERFUCKERS!!!"

Nobody said anything for a second, so Gary moved swiftly, heading for a door at the rear of the gym, a utility room where Gary's band, the No-Names, was allowed to practice once a week.

It was early September 1993. Gary was twenty-five; he'd been down for six years. After stints at Riverside and at Scotts Correctional Facility, he'd been transferred here, to Ryan Regional Correctional Facility, a new maximum-security prison in the middle of bombed-out Detroit. Gary had long hair, a stubbly chin, veiny arms; his trapezius muscles bulged into a hard collar of fleshy mass that jutted up through the deep V neck of his shirt. Every day, rain or sun or snow, he hit the weight pit in the yard, then spent an hour throwing karate kicks against a cement wall. He had gained fifty pounds; the other cons called him Bulldog.

Gary had adapted to prison the best he could, tried to master those parts of his life that were still under his control. He passed the time drawing ornate renderings of women and wolves, wrote letters, prayed. He played cards, read Stephen King. He stopped beating off because wet dreams were better, more real, like you were there. He brushed his teeth six times a day. He hooked up his radio to his guitar amp, a makeshift stereo. He learned how to dance. How to sew. How to make a knife using a toothbrush, a pack of matches, and a disposable razor. How to get himself into a routine, to move slowly and deliberately, to make use of every second. To count the days that passed but never the days that remained.

Over time Gary discovered that prison was, well, put it like this: There was no way you would choose to be here. But once you resigned yourself to being here, and once you resigned yourself to having no control or freedom, prison wasn't all that bad. You could wear your own clothes, work out as much as you wanted, buy bags of fresh-popped popcorn in the yard, touch your people when they came to visit, even have sex in the visiting-room toilet. You could have a

TV and a radio, a typewriter or a sewing machine. For a few years, before they cut the funding, you could go to school and earn college credits. You could work making soap, making cigarettes, operating a forklift, doing laundry, tutoring other prisoners for their GEDs.

The real problem with prison was the prisoners. The dregs of society were in here. They had nothing left to lose. You had to watch out constantly for robbers, confidence men, dangerous psychos. People would split your melon for twenty-five dollars. They'd fuck with you just to have something to do. You had to hold your face a certain way, tough and noncommittal, and your eyes a certain way, askance but all-seeing. You had to watch who you talked to and what you said. You had to learn to sleep lightly, how to rig a nighttime barrier around your bunk. You had to be careful of people who were too friendly. You had to be careful of people who wanted to make you their bitch. You had to be careful of the guards; they ran all sorts of scams. And you had to watch out for gangs—there was constant fighting and racial tension. Overall, you learned to stick with your own, to mind your own business, to keep the faith. And to never, ever be a snitch.

Gary reached the utility room, rushed in, slammed the door.

"Dude, we didn't know if you were going to show," said JK, the lead guitarist in the band. He was sitting in a circle with the others—Big George, Snake Eyes, and Tom; a murderer, an armed robber, and a rapist; on bass, drum machine, and keyboard. Gary was the singer. They covered songs by Metallica, Black Sabbath, Anthrax.

"Look, man, if they rush me in here, you guys just stay out of it," said Gary, picking up a tennis racket, testing the weight.

"No, man," said Tom, the drummer, rising out of this chair, picking up another tennis racket. "If they bust in here, I'm with you, man."

"Dude, you ain't gonna do nothing with me, man," said Gary. He took a practice swing, chopping the air with the racket. "I stand alone. This is my problem."

Gary's problem was tricky. It had started four years ago, with his mom.

For a long time after Gary's conviction, Linda Fannon lived in a fog. She couldn't talk to anyone about her problems; people believed that Gary was a drug kingpin who'd gotten what he deserved. When his appeal was turned down, she considered suicide, but only briefly. Her boy was in prison for life. She had to get him out. The question was how.

Then one day in 1989 Linda heard that Kurt Johnston had been dismissed from the Canton Township police force for using drugs. A quantity of prescriptions drugs had gone missing from the evidence room. The detectives were all screened for drugs. Johnston tested positive for coke and Valium. Though he denied stealing the drugs, he was fired.

All along Linda had believed the cops were crooked. Now she had the evidence. She called Gary's attorney, who wanted more money. She had already spent more than $30,000 on legal fees. She had to try something else.

Linda went to the library and discovered she was not alone; there were groups all across the country fighting state and federal mandatory-minimum drug laws. Michigan's, it turned out, was the toughest in the nation. A study by the *Detroit Free Press* had found that while the statute was intended to snare "drug kingpins," big dealers had largely avoided the Michigan penalties. You had to be caught with more than 3,000 pounds of coke to get life in the federal system. Like Gary, the majority of Michigan's 650 lifers were first-time offenders. More than 50 percent were low-level functionaries—lookouts, drivers, couriers.

Linda called the newspapers and the television stations, contacted William Bryant, a state representative. After many calls and visits from Linda, Bryant was persuaded to hold legislative hearings in Lansing, the state capital. Linda testified. A reporter who worked for the Detroit Free Press was moved by her story. MOTHER TAKES FIGHT AGAINST LIFE SENTENCES TO LEGISLATURE, read the headline on March 18, 1991. "I will fight until the day I die," Linda was quoted as saying. Encouraged, she stepped up her efforts, criss-crossing the state, speaking out.

In the summer of 1992, while researching a story about manda-tory minimums for *Rolling Stone*, I read about Linda and Gary in *USA Today*. I flew to Michigan to meet them and was so struck by their story that I featured only them in my piece.

Following the *Rolling Stone* story, there was a flood of publicity. Linda appeared on a dozen national television talk and newsmagazine shows. Gary appeared too, a disembodied head on a TV monitor. The response was overwhelming—Gary began receiving more than thirty letters a day from all over the world.

A year later, in the summer of 1993, I went to see Gary again. Though he had received a lot of media attention, his situation was unchanged. The drug war was still in full swing. Two bills in the Michigan legislature that Linda had helped bring to fruition were stalled in committee; both the Michigan and the U.S. Supreme Courts had ruled sentences like Gary's constitutional. Gary was still in prison for life. Wanting to help, I wrote a follow-up.

Rolling Stone was well circulated at Ryan, and when that second article appeared, in September 1993, everyone knew about it, though few had read it. The first article had focused on the issue of mandatory minimums; none of the cons had much comment. The second, however, focused on Gary's life inside Ryan. Though I had made an effort to protect him, I had unwittingly committed several errors of judgment. I mentioned in the article that there were gangs and drugs in the prison and that couples fondled in the visiting rooms—the kind of stuff found in every prison movie. I didn't think that I was revealing secrets.

The cons at Ryan thought otherwise.

They believed Gary had written the article himself. And they believed that Gary had broken the ultimate prison code: He was a snitch. A price was put on his life.

The guards came to the utility-room rehearsal hall and cuffed his hands behind his back, led him against his will toward protective custody, the lowest rung of prison hell, the haven of snitches and sissies and child molesters. To reach p.c., the guards had to walk Gary through the main area of the prison, an atrium affair with the cell blocks stacked one on top of the other.

As they entered the room, a guard on either side, the sergeant behind wrenching up Gary's arms, the other prisoners began yelling and spitting and throwing things down from their cells. "There go the snitch!" "Ruff, ruff, ruff, bull bitch." "Cheese eater!"

"FUCK YOU, BITCHES!" screamed Gary. He struggled, staggered, fell to the floor, hit his head. The cons heckled and taunted.

The guards looked at one another and smirked. Gary felt like Jesus walking the last mile. The sergeant hauled him up by his wrists. "Come on, Bulldog, you're making me look bad."

"Hey, Gary, you got any of those nutty bars?"

On a crisp afternoon in November 1995, Gary pulled off his reading glasses and looked up from his typewriter. Some days he spent eight hours at his desk, answering letters, dispensing advice and updates on mandatory minimums to cons in other prisons, helping to organize Friends of Gary Fannon, writing steamy letters to several girls, including his main true love, Alita.

Alita had contacted Gary five years ago, after reading about him. She was doing five to fifteen on charges of vehicular manslaughter. At first Gary and Alita were pen pals. Then, during the two months Gary was locked down in p.c. at Ryan, the tone of the letters began to change. By the time he'd gotten to this new prison, the Lakeland Correctional Facility in Coldwater, they'd declared their mutual love.

Alita was housed at a women's facility a mile from Coldwater. He'd never seen her, never heard her voice. If he went out to the corner of the yard, past the garden, behind the greenhouse and peered across the fields, he could see tiny people in the yard of the women's prison. Once a week, at a special time, he'd go behind the greenhouse with a shard of mirror and reflect the sun. Alita would signal back.

Coldwater was known as a soft place. Many of the prisoners were in for rape or child molestation or had been in p.c. at another facility. Coldwater was in the country, next to an Amish settlement. The buildings had once housed a children's mental hospital.

The relaxed atmosphere at Coldwater, Gary discovered, had an odd by-product—everyone had a business. One guy sold hot dogs and chili dogs; another sold sandwiches stolen from the kitchen. Israel the Rastafarian was a wizard with electronics. There were tattoo artists. Loan sharks. Leather workers. Bookies. Greeting-card makers. Portrait artists. Drug dealers. Spud-juice bootleggers. Hit men. Letter writers. Rip was the store man; he sold cookies, Kool-Aid, razors, same as the prison store. In fact, he bought his merchandise from the prison store. Rip charged one dollar for a seventy-five cent bag of chips. But he was always open. And Rip gave credit, with interest, of course.

A few weeks into his stay, someone asked Gary if he could buy a candy bar for him, and Gary's entrepreneurial instincts stirred. He started with a box of peanut-butter cups, branched out into nutty bars, then Kool-Aid, then chips. He'd spend $100 a week and make thirty or forty dollars profit.

Soon Gary had jars and socks and pockets full of tokens, the coins that were used inside as tender. He cashed them in, sent money home to his mom. He started a loan business and then got an idea for a sort of prison ATM. Someone outside would send Gary's mom a check for fifty dollars, and Gary would dispense thirty-five dollars in tokens to the designated prisoner. His basketball pool, twenty-five cents a ticket, was an immediate success. Then came haircuts, one dollar a head. Typing was twenty-five cents a page.

By November 1995, Gary was living about as well as you could behind bars. He had cons minding his store, collecting his debts, selling basketball tickets. He paid two cons to set the point spread for basketball. Another was paid to run errands. Gary had a big radio, all the sweatpants and T-shirts he could wear. Though he never missed a prison meal—he figured the state owed it to him—he augmented his diet with special food from the kitchen, sandwiches and meats, orange juice, fruit. Even with the scams people were always pulling—like the time his consultants rigged the basketball pool and cleaned him out—he'd sent home in excess of $3,000 during the past year.

Most important, for the first time in years, there was a movement on Gary's case. A dedicated young Detroit attorney, Patrick McQueeney, had managed to persuade Judge Battani to hear new evidence. He'd subpoenaed Kurt Johnston. The date was set.

Now, at his desk in Coldwater on this afternoon in November, eight months before his scheduled hearing, Gary finished a letter to his mom and turned off his electric typewriter. He cocked his head, cut his eyes upward, toward his customer. "I don't know about any more nutty bars, Lindsey. What about your girlish figure?"

"Oh Gary, don't you know it's not polite to talk about a lady's weight?" Lindsey laughed, her voice coy and smoky. She had long, straight blond hair and big breasts. Her shirt was tied up in a little knot to expose her doughy midriff. She went about five feet seven, 160 pounds, said her name was Lindsey Starr, headlining female impersonator at all the great rooms in Vegas and L.A., best known for her Julie Andrews and her Ann-Margret.

After nine years in prison, Gary knew well that sissies could mean big trouble. But Coldwater was sissy heaven. There were guys sucking dicks everywhere in the shadows. There were super-sissies all over the yard with big-time makeup and poofed hair. Some of them had implants in their cheeks and chins and hips, and the shit had melted or something, and they looked like monsters. It was a freak show, you know. Gary was fascinated.

When Lindsey first started coming around, however, Gary refused to even look at her. In all these years, he'd never thought of doing any gay stuff. To tell the truth, the thing he missed the most was spooning: He dreamed of lying in bed with Alita, her arms wrapped around him.

Lindsey chased after Gary. She frequented his store, quizzed him about the basketball pool. She watched him lift weights, made comments about his body. One day Gary got fed up. He pinned her neck against the wall. "CUT IT THE FUCK OUT OR I'LL RIP YOUR HEAD OFF!" he roared.

Lindsey got the message, sort of. Though she kept coming around, she softened her approach. Slowly, the two began to talk. Gary asked her why she was the way she was, and she told him the whole story about being a little girl stuck in a little boy's body. She was about forty years old, and she was real attractive when her makeup was on, this tan eye makeup with the light brown eyes—it was nice.

Over time Lindsey became a fixture in Gary's routine. He'd be out in the yard with his friend Eric, or they'd be playing cards or pool, and Lindsey would be hanging around, sitting off to one side with her legs crossed just so. It was like being on the outside again, having a woman around. As Lindsey used to say, she was one slice away from being a real girl.

Lindsey was funny. She acted out little dramas, snapped her fingers in the air, did different voices. She told stories about her days onstage. She told stories about Zebra, her current lover. They called him Zebra because he had these weird patches of gray hair. Zebra was in love with Lindsey. He cleaned up her room, cleaned the mud off her shoes, followed her around, kept trying to get her alone in the shower. He had offered to transfer $1,500 into Lindsey's prison account if she'd tell everyone he was her husband.

One day in the yard, Gary and Eric were playing cards and Lindsey was hanging around. Zebra was across the way, bellowing. It was his birthday. He wanted Lindsey. "Get away from those motherfuckers!" he hollered.

Lindsey rolled her eyes. Gary and Eric laughed.

"Fuck you!" screamed Zebra. He stormed across the yard.

Gary set himself in a T stance. "You don't have to go nowhere you don't want to, Lindsey," said Gary.

"Not while we're still standing," said Eric.

"Fuck you, motherfuckers," said Zebra.

"Boys, boys, boys!" sang Lindsey, stepping between her knights, looking very pleased. She took Zebra by the elbow, aimed him across the yard. "See you guys later!" she sang over her shoulder.

Life went on, the whole incident pretty much forgotten. Then, about a week later, Linda Fannon received an anonymous letter from Coldwater. It said Gary and Lindsey were lovers. "This is gonna mess up your chances to get out, Gary," Linda sobbed over the telephone.

Gary was furious. He told his mom to get real. "Mail me that letter," he said.

The evidence arrived a few days later. Gary gave it to Lindsey, who checked it against her trove of greeting cards and love letters, kept in a shoebox tied with a lace ribbon. Now, as Gary handed her a nutty bar, she told him she'd come up with a match. "It was Shorty," Lindsey concluded.

Shorty was a little Black guy, five feet four, a closet sissy who hung around with all the gang members who had recently started flowing into Coldwater. Shorty was friends with Zebra. He was also in love with Lindsey.

Gary found Shorty in a hallway near the gym, talking to one of his boys. Gary leaned against the opposite wall, a few feet away, and commenced staring at Shorty, giving him what they call a marquette—a hard, menacing glare.

He stared at Shorty, marquetting him, marquetting the little fucker. Finally, Shorty turned to Gary: "You got a problem?"

"Yeah, I got a fuckin' problem."

They went into the weight room. "Sit down," he commanded Shorty.

"I don't want to sit down."

"SIT DOWN, BITCH, BEFORE I KNOCK YOU DOWN!"

Shorty sat down.

"Now, listen here, you motherfucker," Gary said calmly. "If my mother ever gets another letter..."

"I didn't write no letters!" whined Shorty.

"Shut up, BITCH!" said Gary. He jabbed Shorty in the chest with his first two fingers—a hard, tight poke. Shorty tumbled backward off the bench, onto the floor.

"You gonna put your hands on me now, huh, is that it?" whined Shorty.

"Bitch, you're lucky I don't strangle your ass. If my mother gets another letter, I'm gonna kill you. I'm gonna fucking butcher you. I'm gonna drag your motherfuckin' dead carcass up to the control center, and I'm gonna spit on you as I walk. NOW GET THE FUCK OUT OF MY FACE!"

A half hour later, Shorty was back. He had his boys behind him, five of them, and a tile-cutting knife, sharp and curved, in his hand. He found Gary in the yard with Eric.

Shorty advanced toward Gary, slashing the air with the knife, making kung fu noises. Gary wrapped his sweatshirt around his arm, assumed a T stance.

Shorty lunged. Gary blocked with his sweatshirt. Shorty lunged. Gary blocked with a side kick. A crowd gathered. "Kill that White motherfucker!" "Butcher that nigger!" Shorty slashed, a wild swing.

Gary backed up, backed up. He felt like a punk. He outweighed Shorty by a hundred pounds. He could take the knife, break his wrist. He could kill the little fucker with a snap kick or a roundhouse to the temple or the jaw. But he didn't know what to do. *I could blow my chances for a new trial!*

Shorty lunged.

Fuck it, thought Gary. He did a fancy spin, planted his front foot. He ran away.

Gary sat on his bunk with his head bowed, trying not to think. It was a muggy afternoon, a month before his twenty-eighth birthday.

Gary had been down now for just under ten years. Six weeks ago, he'd finally had his trial, a four-day hearing on his "motion for relief from judgment" before the same judge who had sent him away. At this very moment—2:05 p.m., July 25, 1996—in Wayne County Circuit Court, 150 highway miles west of Coldwater, Judge Marianne Battani was ready to deliver her oral decision.

In the front row of the gallery, Linda Fannon was surrounded by family, coworkers, supporters, journalists, a carload of nuns in habit. Linda had dreamed of this day for years. No matter what happened now, at least she could finally say that the truth had come out.

Gary's original trial attorney had testified that he was a general practitioner who dabbled in criminal law. He said he had never discussed an entrapment defense with Gary because he didn't believe there were grounds.

Gary's appeals attorney had testified that, based on his review of Gary's trial record, he had believed that entrapment was not a viable option for Gary's appeal, even after Kurt Johnston had been dismissed for using drugs.

Several of Gary's old friends had testified that Gary had never done or sold coke before meeting Johnston.

Patrick McQueeney had grilled Johnston for three hours. Johnston, who had become a drug counselor after leaving the police force, denied snorting coke with Gary. He denied skimming coke off the top of drug deals. He admitted to testing positive for coke use, explaining that he'd sometimes rubbed a little on his gums to relieve certain aches and pains and that he had snorted it while working cases. Johnston also testified that he had no knowledge of Gary ever dealing coke before he himself started Gary off.

Now, in the Wayne County Circuit courtroom, the judge began delivering her oral opinion. "This court has certainly been involved with this case for a long time. It has a long and tortured history."

Linda sat on the hard bench, trying to concentrate. She sat there, listening but not listening, watching the burnished red lips of this portly woman as she spoke from her seat high over the courtroom.

Finally, Linda could hear summation in the judge's voice. She tuned back in.

"Given all these factors," the judge was saying, "the court finds that the defendant was entrapped into committing these crimes. The court further finds that trial counsel for defendant was ineffective, and of course there is ineffective assistance of appellate counsel. The court hereby sets aside the conviction of Mr. Fannon."

Pandemonium. Linda laid her head on the rail and began to cry. Everyone else stood at their seats, clapping and cheering. Even the judge broke a smile.

"Gary?" called Linda. "What are you doing?"

It was well after midnight, his first day back in the world. The light was bright and harsh. Gary's hands were buried in his pants pockets. His eyes were glazed.

"What is it, Gary?"

"Look," he said, sweeping a palm along the vista before him, two nine-foot-high rows of shelves—the cereal aisle at the supermarket.

They'd come here because they weren't tired yet and needed a few things for the morning and because, well, just because they could. Entering the store, they went first to the cereal aisle. Linda left him there, told him to pick out something he liked. Gary scanned the shelves. There was Raisin Bran, Bran Chex, Shredded Wheat, Frosted Wheat-Bites, Frosted Mini-Wheats, Quaker, Post, Kellogg's, Nature Valley. Low fat, no fat, no sodium, high fiber, high vitamin. In prison they plopped oatmeal on your plate. You ate it.

Linda came back twenty minutes later, her cart brimming. Gary was standing exactly where she'd left him.

She smiled indulgently and tousled his forelock, the way she used to do when he stood waist high. "Here," she said, reaching for a box. "You used to like Frosted Flakes."

Since he walked out of Coldwater late Friday afternoon, July 26, 1996, to the cheers of friends and family and even the press, things have been a little bumpy for Gary. As Linda said, "He's like a child, discovering the whole big, wide world." The minute he arrived at Linda's apartment, the phone began ringing, and he literally ran to answer it. He hadn't answered a phone in almost ten years.

Gary had been sent away at eighteen—a damaged, troubled, good-natured boy just out of high school. He came of age inside prison, learned the ropes, built a life, got along the best he could. Rather than let prison corrupt him, he worked on himself, tried hard to be honest, loyal, thrifty, and brave, a Boy Scout among the infidels. He had always believed God gave you what you deserved, good or bad. Gary figured he deserved to go to prison for all the things he'd done wrong in his life. He saw his stretch as his penance, an opportunity to earn a second chance, to travel a different path than he might have. He discovered over time that if you try hard enough to be something, you grow into it.

The Gary Fannon who emerged from a decade behind bars is today a fine and simple man, naïve about the ways of business and social intercourse and grown-up women, an odd combination of coarsened ex-con and earnest young man, Jacobo Timerman meets Forrest Gump. Within days of his release, he was working for his lawyer as a gofer. He is now attending Schoolcraft College in Livonia in the hope of becoming a physical therapist. After the first semester, he posted a 3.6 average. He also works the midnight shift as an order selector in a food distributor's warehouse; he became full-time after only nine weeks, a record for the company.

After a brief fling with Alita when he first got home—she'd been out a year, was six months pregnant and separated from her new husband—Gary got together with a young single mom. He's not sure of their future yet, but in the meantime he's settled into the complex, befuddling institution that is modern domesticity.

Gary has been to several lawyers about suing the state of Michigan, the police, Kurt Johnston, someone. Three different lawyers have passed, saying he has no case. Meanwhile he works all night long, goes to school in the morning, sleeps in the early evening, reports to work at midnight. He is tired. He is stressed out. He is stressed out about being stressed out. He feels as though he should be happy all the time now that he's free. He's learning that freedom brings complications.

"I'm pretty happy, I guess," says Gary. "But it seems like I'm still waiting. For ten years, I waited to be free. Now I'm waiting to get what's mine, what I deserve in life. At first I didn't feel like I was robbed. I was just glad to be out. But now I'm starting to look around at these other twenty-eight-year-old guys, and they have the wife, the kids, the house, all the good stuff. It's like I'm struggling to get to a place where I should already be. I think a lot about those ten years I lost. I'm trying to appreciate what I have. Let me tell you, bud. It ain't easy."

REVENGE OF THE DONUT BOYS

Newark, New Jersey, once had the highest rate of car theft in the nation, 56 percent of which were perpetrated by teens and preteens. Sometimes the kids were so young it took two to drive—one worked the pedals, the other the wheel.

At midday in summer haze the basketballs are bouncing in a playground surrounded by a chain-link fence. From here, on a little hill behind Avon Elementary, Newark, New Jersey, stretches in all directions: the Gothic spires of abandoned churches, the dense brick towers of the projects, the ghost buildings boarded with plywood. Liquor stores, Korean markets, garages, vast tracts of vacant land, acre upon acre of weeds mulched with broken glass and needles and little vials and shell casings, blood dripped and dried brown on chips of brick and concrete, the rubble of housing and commerce and people.

Little kids dart across the asphalt playground, stumbling here and there on tufts of stubborn grass. Bigger kids on corners reach for pockets, shake hands. Women lean out windows, girls gossip on porches, old men hunker at salvaged card tables, drinking from paper bags. Now and then comes a *pop-pop-pop* and a rolling echo, the crack and thunder of far-off gunplay. No one pays it any mind.

That corner to the north is known for marijuana. Over there you get pills, over there heroin, over there crack, over there powder. The shadow economy working overtime, mutant enterprise blooming amid the ruins of a city that was the leading supplier of manufactured goods to the South before the Civil War. MADE IN NEWARK once meant patent leather and tools. Now it means kids like Raheed.

Raheed isn't his real name. He wants to stay on the super DL, meaning he'll talk, but only with his head down low, incognito. He wears a bandanna on his head folded and tied in the back. His short pants ride low on his hips, hang below his knees. He leans on crutches, eating his breakfast, a bag of chips.

Suddenly from up Avon comes the roar of engines, and two black Mustangs and a Honda crest the hill. People scurry across the street, girls laugh and point. The cars whiz past the school-yard, each one driven by a boy barely tall enough to see over the steering wheel, each one full of boys, five or six or more, the Honda with two heads in backward baseball caps grinning up through the sunroof. Games cease on the playground. Kids run to the fence. The Mustangs speed through the intersection at sixty, bottom out with a clank, shed sparks, zoom off. The Honda hits the crosswalk, turns hard left, squeals and slides and then spins in the center of the intersection, tires screaming, leaving rubber, raising clouds of thick black smoke that envelop the car, waft off on the humid breeze.

"The Doughnut Boys!" shout the children. They clap and cheer. They do a little dance called the Doughnut, spin round and round and round.

In America's third oldest major city, a new sport has been born. It's called rustling cars. According to auto-theft statistics, Newark has the highest rate of car theft per capita in the nation, more than forty cars each day. Sixty-five percent of the thefts are perpetrated by teens and preteens, known hereabout as the Doughnut Boys.

The Doughnut Boys steal Hondas, Acuras, Mustangs, Trans Ams, four-wheelers, and minivans: the same models you might see in a high school parking lot in the nearby suburbs. They use screwdrivers to jack the door and punch the steering column. They override kill switches and alarms. Fifteen seconds, tops. High craft, handed down from brother to friend.

They'll rustle up a car to drive to elementary school, in lieu of bus fare, to get out of the rain, for a date, a purse snatching, a cruise around town, a drug delivery, sometimes an armed robbery. They steal from garages, alleyways, curbs. Not long ago, someone stole the county prosecutor's car from a schoolyard. He was inside addressing an assembly on the subject of stealing cars.

One kid steals a car, picks up some friends, drives to Newark Airport or the suburbs. The friends jump out and steal cars of their own. With the little ones, it takes two to drive. One gets the pedals, the other the wheel. Then it's a race back to the neighborhood, where the fun begins.

Pull up beside a cop, flip him the finger, peel off. The kids know five-o ain't allowed to race: High-speed chase is outlawed. Race them anyway. Turn right, right again, bust the lights, weave the lanes, Mario Andretti. Dick the cops. That's the object: Smoke 'em. Humiliate 'em. Fuck 'em up. Chicken at sixty miles per hour, stolen Honda heading straight for patrol car. The cops always veer off at the last moment. Pussies. No match. Recently, the Doughnut Boys have added a new wrinkle. Ram a patrol car. See the air bags pop.

"It's a big show," says Raheed. He's seventeen. He's been down to juvenile, but now he's back. He broke his leg the other night fleeing on foot from a stolen car. "It's the most exciting thing going on in the neighborhood. It's like the movies, you know what I'm sayin'? Car chases. Everybody like to see cars spinning and stuff. Everybody want to get in a car.

"When you down in the hood and shit, straight up, preachin' high, we down here trapped off among ourselves. It's like little kids in the hood throw rocks. Then they be stealing cars. Whereas in Short Hills, they might be playing golf. But this is the hood. These are the things that we do for activities. That calms ourselves. It's a recreation-type thing. Like, they got the playground open now. Tomorrow, boom, it's Saturday. It ain't gonna be open. What we gonna do then? You know what I'm sayin'? Fuck it. Let's go get a car. It's like—"

"Shut up, crook!" says a kid on a bicycle. His name is Rico. He's ten.

"Fuck you!" says Raheed. He swings a crutch at Rico's front tire. Rico holds his ground astride his bike, safely out of range. "Fuck yourself," he says. "You ain't got nothin' better to do than try to steal somebody else's car that they done paid for."

"Oh, you a good Samaritan," says Raheed, "you bike stealer little faggot-ass motherfucker. Stop playing me out!"

"Shut up, nigga!"

"Shut up, punk!"

Raheed hops toward the boy, brandishing a crutch. Rico backs off slowly, giggling, taunting. A teacher appears. Ms. Perkins is the drug-education coordinator for Avon Elementary. The city pays her to keep the playground open on summer afternoons. When her car was stolen, she put out the word. Kids from all over were calling the cops with sightings of her white Sunbird. She got it back in a few hours. She puts a hand on Raheed's shoulder. "What's up, gentlemen?"

Over the last year or so, hundreds of kids from Newark have been injured and arrested, and millions of dollars' worth of cars have been stolen. Not long ago, a fourteen-year-old took out half a gas station pulling up to the pump. A pregnant woman was killed when the police fired into a stolen van. In late August, two teenagers on a 4:00 a.m. rustle were shot to death after encountering a pair of off-duty policemen. Cops have been injured, too. Herded to the curbs by teams of unmarked police cars and trucks, the kids have taken to ramming. Back and forth they bang, trying to break a piece of daylight for escape. As the kids become increasingly defiant—most of them are juveniles who will likely be released—the cops grow increasingly frustrated.

So it was this past June when Howard "Bucky" Caesar had the bad fortune to be caught driving a stolen black IROC-Z Camaro belonging to the mother of a Newark police officer. Bucky was doing doughnuts at four in the morning when he lost control of the Camaro and slammed into the curb, breaking an axle. Already there had been reports of Newark cops hiding in the bushes at a local park, throwing rocks and bottles as the Doughnut Boys sped past in stolen cars. Now, when Bucky jumped out of the Camaro on the morning of June 9 to the jeers and catcalls of bystanders at the all-night show, it was gunfire that the police were throwing down. Bucky was hit in the side.

Six cops were on the scene, some of whom weren't assigned to the area. The son of the owner of the stolen Camaro arrived shortly thereafter. The police reported the shooting to headquarters at 4:41 a.m. The car was reported stolen at 4:42. Witnesses reported the police retrieving spent shell casings. In their reports, only one officer admitted firing shots. He and two others have been charged with failing to report the shooting and filing false reports. All six have been suspended. Bucky remains in stable condition after eight operations.

In a city that is a model of urban statistical cliché, Bucky Caesar grew up something of an anomaly, with a mother and father and two siblings at home. His dad was a janitor for the Newark schools. They lived in the ghetto because it was all they could afford, five rooms for $400 a month.

Their neighborhood around Twentieth Street was once known for heroin and pills. Later it would be crack, then guns, then stolen cars. "We didn't need no VCR," says Bucky's mom, Martha Caesar. "Everyone and everything was out there."

"I didn't really feel scared, though," says Caesar, who has since moved. "I like the people down there. I didn't like what they did, but we all stuck together as family. I lived on the third floor, so they couldn't climb through the window, but I had no fear of anyone kickin' in my door or robbin' me, either. I had my husband and my kids. Mr. C. was like a father figure to everyone before he died, rest his soul. He'd get out there in the fire hydrant on hot summer nights with all the kids."

As it was, Mr. C.'s younger son had problems of his own, beginning early on in school. There was the second-grade teacher who smacked him, family counseling, more acting up in class. By the time he got to high school, Bucky was classified as emotionally disturbed. "It made him feel like he was dumb and retarded," says Martha Caesar.

Soon Bucky started stealing cars, and finally he found something he was pretty good at. In fact, he was out of control. One minute he would be out front with his friends. The next he'd be gone. What could Martha Caesar do? When she asked, Bucky said he did it for status, as if stealing the symbols of accomplishment of the middle class raised him up into it. What he couldn't obtain, he just took and used and destroyed.

"You instill in your child what is right and wrong," says Caesar. "But you can't be out there twenty-four seven. The word of God tell us to bring a child up in the right way, and when he get old, he shall not depart from that teaching. But it doesn't say nothing about between the time you train him and the time he get old. He has to get some years on him, some wisdom to know what his parents tell him is true. God help him in the meantime."

"He a car thief," says Rico, spitting out the charge, explaining the sudden flare-up on the playground to Ms. Perkins. "Every time he get locked up, he like 'Pleassse, go get my ma!'"

"That's right, motherfucker," says Raheed. "And you see I be out the next day."

"I ain't never been locked up," says Rico. Standing there astride his bike, between Raheed and Ms. Perkins, he crosses his arms, cocks a hip, assumes a pose of proud defiance.

Ms. Perkins smiles to herself, lets the show run. Rico is one of her favorites. So delicate, with long lashes, yet hardy enough somehow to survive. Ms. Perkins has worked on that boy for four years. He's like so many kids she knows. The children of lost children, little renegades on the loose. His mother's never home, doesn't care where he's at. His brother's a car thief. Rico isn't so much a member of a family as he is a resident of a house. Maybe that's why all these kids use the word *stay* instead of *live* when they talk about home. "I stay over at Clinton Avenue" is how they put it.

Ms. Perkins comes from the neighborhood. She doesn't like what she sees, but that's how it is. She includes in her job description the role of surrogate parent. The government won't do it. The parents won't either. She's spent four years trying to teach Rico things like decision making and refusal skills, responsibilities, goals, and directions. She wasn't sure she was getting through. Now, here on the playground, she sees a sprout on one of the seeds she's planted. Just when you think they're not thinking, they're thinking, and you're surprised.

"Why you want to steal those cars anyway?" Ms. Perkins asks Raheed.

"Why?" repeats Raheed, folding his arms across his chest, striking a pose of his own. "Lemme tell you serious. We do it to help society."

"Yeah?"

"Yeah," says Raheed. "Because if it wasn't for us, you wouldn't have no hospitals and police. Word is born. We employ the fuckin' police!" Raheed's voice begins to rise, his words do a dance of rhythmic hip-hop. He hobbles back and forth, a crippled rapper on an asphalt stage. A group of little ones have gathered to see the show, more of Ms. Perkins's kids: Rashonda and Dwane and Hassan, Jennifer and Sade, Aliyah and Tony. They are four, five, ten years old. They hold basketballs and jump ropes, the sticky hands of younger cousins.

"Word is born!" says Raheed, playing to his Sesame Street crowd. "If it wasn't for niggas like me, a lot of families be starvin' 'cause they husbands'll get laid the fuck off, because it ain't no crime. And what about insurance? The insurance companies be worth, like, billions of dollars and stuff. They wouldn't be nowhere without us."

"You oughta run for president," giggles Rico. The other kids giggle, too.

"I thought of it, but I ain't goin' out like that," says Raheed, talking serious. "I don't even know what the sense of voting in the first place. Ain't none of them crackers for none of us."

"You gotta be about yourself," says Ms. Perkins. "Being about yourself mean getting some education. You sound like you not stupid."

"You got that right," says Raheed. "I got friends that graduated outta high school, and boom, word is born! They working at McDonald's. What's up with that?"

"But they workin'," says Ms. Perkins.

"So what," says Raheed. "I got my equivalency, too. I don't want no job."

"What about a decent job? Maybe like a computer programmer?"

"I don't want no decent job."

"So you to the point where you don't want no job at all," says Ms. Perkins.

"I never did want no job."

Ms. Perkins puts a hand on her hip, gives Raheed a look, part patience and humor, part disgust. "What are you, about seventeen now, boyfriend?" Raheed nods. "Okay. Now I know what seventeen is like, so I ain't gonna press the issue on that. But look. You got maybe sixty more years to live. What you gonna do with that time?"

"I wanna rap," says Raheed.

"You wanna rap," repeats Ms. Perkins.

"You wanna die!" pipes Rico. He giggles. So do the kids.

Ms. Perkins falls quiet. A light turns off in her pleasant, sunny face. She looks around her. Rashonda and Dwane, Hassan and Jennifer, Sade, Aliyah and Tony. Four, five, ten years old, basketballs and jump-ropes and sticky hands. And Rico, posing there astride his bike. "Does he really mean it?" she asks herself. "Have I gotten through?" There are so many kids like Rico. So many more kids than time. In the middle distance, she can hear the piercing rubber squeal of a Doughnut Boy, another lost renegade soul spinning around in circles on a ghetto street in Newark. She wonders what will happen tomorrow. On Saturday the playground is closed.

DEATH IN VENICE

Back in the day, when gangs fought for turf and respect, V-13 ruled the streets of Venice, California—proud *vatos* in their Pendleton shirts and hairnets. They drove shiny lowriders and sold heroin to the *miatas*, the poor Blacks across the street. Then crack arrived in the neighborhood and the tables turned. Life inside an L.A. gang.

Lil' Sleeper and Margarita are hanging out at Yogi's, all three sitting on his bed. The room is dark, narrow, smoky. A towel is jammed against the bottom of the door.

"I forgot to tell you," Yogi says. "Sleeper called."

"Yeah?" asks Lil' Sleeper.

"He asked what have we done to pay back Culver City."

"Pay 'em back for what?"

"You know, man. The drive-by at the park. Those *vatos* who shot at us. Remember, *ese*?"

Lil' Sleeper chews his thumb and thinks for a minute. The TV flickers, the radio plays rap, a table fan moves air back and forth. He turns to Margarita, his girlfriend. "When this happen?"

Margarita's eyes pan slowly toward his face. They've been dating for a year. She is wearing a black miniskirt and a necklace of hickeys, a pair of three-inch heels she bought two weeks ago on her fourteenth birthday. Her hair is shoulder length, crowned at the front with a stiff pompadour—a four-inch tiara of bangs combed skyward and encased in Aqua Net hairspray. She blinks. She shrugs. She don't remember, either. One day be like the next.

Lil' Sleeper chews his thumb some more. The skin at the tip, just below the nail, is burned and crusty, a condition the homeboys call Bic Thumb. Like Yogi, he is nineteen. He is wearing a nylon sweat suit and high-top Adidas. His hair is black as tar, clipped short and oiled straight back from a widow's peak. His lashes are long and curly, his eyes are bloodshot, one of his front teeth is missing. The first time he was arrested he was six years old; he stole a TV from his grammar school. Last year, he was arrested eleven times for being under the influence of heroin and two times for being under the influence of PCP, a drug he likes because "when you do it, it be hard for you to walk and think."

As days in the neighborhood go, this one started off pretty well. At ten this morning, Lil' Sleeper and Margarita ran into a crack dealer they know. He kicked down some love, gave them some free drugs, the dregs of last night's stash—a couple of five- and ten-dollar rocks and a bunch of crumbs. The pair went immediately to Yogi's place and smoked it all in fifteen minutes. Now they need more.

Sitting on the edge of the bed, Lil' Sleeper is a ramrod. His mouth is pulled back in a tight grimace. Above his lip, among the faint stirrings of a mustache, are little drops of sweat. His teeth are clenched; you can see the strain in the muscles of his jaw and in the cords of his neck, upon which is tattooed, in big blue letters, the logo of his gang, V-13.

He plucks an ice cube from his glass, holds it up, regards it in the light. "Wouldn't you like a rock this size?" He sounds like a kid wishing for a pony for his birthday—which in fact he did when he was ten.

"*Yea-ah!*" Yogi enthuses.

"How big would you say this was, a fifty?" Lil' Sleeper asks.

"A righteous five-oh," Yogi opines.

Lil' Sleeper loses himself in his daydream; hope pops like a flashbulb in his eyes, and then the light recedes. His attention drifts to the carpet. There are lots of little white pieces of paper and lint and cloth and cigarette ash down there. To him, each piece looks like a rock. Could be a rock. He has an urge to reach down with his index finger and feel around for *pedasos*, little pieces of crack cocaine. That he *knows* there are no *pedasos* on the carpet, that he's way too methodical to have dropped anything, doesn't matter at all, because something strong makes him want to get down on his hands and knees on the filthy rug in the dark, musky, narrow room and touch each little piece of paper and lint and cloth and ash and test its composition. There are no crumbs. He knows that. It doesn't matter. A few minutes ago, he tried to smoke a sesame seed. It tasted like burnt toast when he fired it up in his pipe, which is really a piece of broken-off car antenna stuffed with ChoreBoy brand copper scouring sponge—the kind without the soap. A recent letter in a local weekly paper complained about the recent epidemic of broken car antennas. Now you know.

"So what are we going to do about Culver City?" Yogi asks. "Sleeper say that if we down for the neighborhood, we gotta pay them back."

Lil' Sleeper looks up from the floor. He and Yogi are members of the Venice Gang, among the oldest and most proud of the 400 gangs in Los Angeles. For more than thirty years, Chicano homeboys have claimed this neighborhood, one square mile of palm trees and poverty in the middle of Venice, California, a little piece of ghetto encrusted in the heart of the California lifestyle like plaque in an artery—long established, nearly impossible to dislodge. Ten years ago, when Yogi and Lil' Sleeper were still playing with toys, war was raging in the neighborhood; V-13 was locked in epic battles with all the gangs surrounding—Santa Monica, Culver City, the Shoreline Crips, the Black gang with whom they share Oakwood, the official name for the section of Venice in which they live. At the time, the *Los Angeles Times* devoted a special section to the unrest. "DEATH, DAILY VIOLENCE BECOME WAY OF LIFE FOR NEIGHBORHOOD," said the headline, one of twelve screamers in the twelve-page pullout. The Los Angeles police department's now-infamous CRASH unit (Community Resources Against Street Hoodlums) cut its teeth in Venice; the National Guard walked the streets for a period, too. A whole generation of Venice homeboys went to jail, became addicted to heroin, or died.

These days, Venice still gets its CRASH sweeps: low-key Tuesday and Thursday night affairs. The *pop-pop-pop* of automatic-weapons fire is still part of the everyday soundtrack of squealing tires, cursing homeboys, laughing children, and thumping rap. But aside from Popo—a homeboy who lost his cool during a burglary and slit the throat of L.A. city councilwoman Ruth Galanter—Venice hasn't been in the news at all lately. South Central Los Angeles is where the action is now. There, Black gangs have adopted the gangsta lifestyle pioneered by the Mexican *cholos* of yore; they have begun a reign of entrepreneurial terror that has turned the L.A. gang culture inside out. For generations, the poor and the powerless of Southern California— as in every urban center across the world—banded together to form neighborhood self-protection societies. They fought for the safety of their streets and for some measure of self-respect. Back in the day, in Los Angeles, the Chicanos were ascendant. Gangs like V-13 were strong and proud.

Today, gangs are no longer about turf and respect. Instead, they are about drugs and money. Crack has done to V-13 what the police and the National Guard and other gangs have been trying to do for years.

Now, in Yogi's room, Lil' Sleeper grinds his teeth some more. He looks beseechingly at his homie: "You think you can get twenty bucks from your moms?"

"*My* moms?" asks Yogi. "What about yours?"

"I asked her yesterday, *ese.*"

They both look at Margarita.

***

The drive-by happened two nights ago.

Yogi, Lil' Sleeper, and Margarita were there, and so were Wormy, Linda, and a couple more *vatos* and *heinas*, dudes and chicks. They were kickin' it on a grassy field behind Broadway Elementary, hunkered in the middle of their own neighborhood, their home turf. Someone had brought a couple *pistos*, big bottles of Colt 45 malt liquor. Someone had some *yeska*, Mexican marijuana, ditch weed. Four of the homies were *shermed*, high on *frios*, which are menthol cigarettes dipped in a bottle of liquid PCP—two of them were crawling around on all fours, unable to walk. Yogi, Lil' Sleeper, Panther, and a White guy named Mike, your reporter, were taking turns crouching behind a wall, doing blasts, taking hits of crack.

Right around midnight, Wormy was smoking another *frio*. Loud and grandiose, he was telling everyone about the time in jail he was stabbed in the head. After that, he began talking about his father, a White man who had abandoned his mom. When the *frio* was finished, he got very quiet. His face assumed a strange, tortured expression.

And then he went *off*.

He smashed a bottle on the sidewalk, uttered incantations to the devil, danced around in the grass. He locked his focus on the White guy who was among them and stood over me and shook his fists. "Prejudice!" he bellowed, over and over. I tried to remain calm and still. At last, Yogi and Lil' Sleeper tackled him. No matter how fucked up they were, during the six weeks I was with them, my guys always had my back.

After a few minutes, things got mellow again. Everybody was chillin', smokin' out, drinkin', having a laugh.

And then, out of the darkness came a souped-up '65 Chevy, white on blue with mag wheels. It squealed around the corner. Shots rang out: quick loud pops from a semiautomatic. From the sound of it, a .22-caliber.

The rounds sizzled the air above our heads. Small bullets can do a lot of damage; they get inside your body and ping around, tearing up organs. Yogi rolled on top of Linda. Margarita rolled on top of Lil' Sleeper. Everyone else hit the dirt.

And then it was over.

A single taillight receded from their territory. In the nighttime stillness, you could hear hoots of laughter coming from the car.

"There go those motherfuckers from Culver City," somebody said.

"Cheese eaters!" Yogi yelled.

"*Putos!*"

Margarita pointed in the opposite direction across the field.

It was Sleeper. He did not look pleased.

Twenty-seven years old, Sleeper is an OG, an original gangsta, one of the leaders in the hood. There are no elected officials in V-13; in a gang, a leader makes himself. Rank is bestowed naturally, over the course of time, by dint of service, reputation, and personality.

Sleeper has a thick scar across this cheek, two bullet holes in his side, another in his shoulder. To this day, he carries a shotgun pellet in his penis. He calls it his Mexican tickler. "What the fuck was that?" he screamed at his young homies.

"Just some of those cheese eaters from Culver City," Yogi said matter-of-factly.

"*Those* motherfuckers? Again?"

Nobody said a word. The two who had earlier been nonambulatory were now passed out on the grass.

Sleeper shook his head sadly. Lately, he thinks, everything is fucked up in the neighborhood. Everything has changed. These younger homeboys know as well as he does what the code is: If someone disrespects you—if he calls you a name, if he mad-dogs you, if he owes you money, if he shoots at you, if he talks shit about your old lady, if he makes you angry about anything at all—there is only one thing you're supposed to do. You go get your gun out of its hiding place, you hunt him down, you cap him, you bust a grape. Or if you can't find *him*, you cap one of his homeboys. You don't drive by—that's for cheese eaters, something else new in the picture. For years the homies from Venice and Culver City have been shooting each other, but it was always done face to face. That was always the rule. Yes, there were *rules*. A code of honor if you will: You don't shoot from a car. You don't shoot at a house. You don't do things to jeopardize innocent children or family members. A few years ago, one of the Venice homeboys took a shot at a rival gang member who was standing outside a church. A mother and her child were killed. As soon as they heard what happened, the Venice homeboys beat up their own *vato*. He was banished from the neighborhood.

Sleeper looked off in the direction the Chevy had retreated. He hocked a fat lugie on the ground. "Somebody better do something soon—or *all* y'all gonna have to deal with *me*."

***

Since 1905, when "Venice of America" was built, complete with canals, as a sort of residential theme park by the Pacific Ocean, the territory just adjacent, called Oakwood, has been poor and predominantly nonwhite, a little patch of blight along the pricey Southern California coast. The older families living in Oakwood date back four or five generations, though the notion of generations can be deceptive here. Many of the women become pregnant at fifteen or sixteen; thirty-year-old grandmothers are not difficult to find.

The neighborhood claimed by V-13 is a ramshackle collection of bungalows with front and back yards. Invariably, there will be one or more older-model Chevrolets around the properties, in various states of disrepair, and maybe an old stove in the back yard. Women who work outside the neighborhood tend to drive small Japanese imports. The walls of all the buildings and fences are covered with graffiti, colorful and riotous tags that identify the gang and its members by their street names—each gang and each man has, in effect, his own logo.

Inside, the houses are tidy and clean; the furnishings and knick-knacks are inexpensive but lovingly kept. Wedding, graduation, and post-boot camp military portraits of family members are displayed high on the walls, above the typical sightline, lending the pictures an iconic air. The television burns twenty-four seven; the electronic hearth is always on. Typically, there is a large living room with lots of sofas and chairs. The seating is plush and comfortable—in general, the dwellers are a substantial lot, owing to a diet heavy with lard and tortillas and sweets; in the eat-in kitchen, there is always an iron skillet of beans on the stove, fresh tortillas on the table. Every other room, including the back porch, is used as a bedroom. People will also sleep at night in the living room.

Typically, four or five generations of relatives live in one house. Great-grandma shares a bedroom with Auntie. Grandma and an orphaned great-niece will share another room. A high-ranking daughter—often the one with the best job—will have a room to herself. A young couple will also have a room. If they have a small child, the child will often sleep with the ranking female. The females of the clan share an elaborate and interwoven network of responsibilities. Everyone cooks, cleans, and takes care of the kids. Young couples have the fewest responsibilities. They are encouraged to sleep late, to make more babies. The older children take care of the younger children. They grow up taking care of one another. One sixteen-year-old mother, when asked about her status as an "unwed mother," knit her brows in puzzlement. "I been taking care of babies since I was five or six," she giggled. "I love babies. I don't see it as a *bad* thing."

The women run the household with a loving but firm hand. Grandma or Great-grandma holds the lease; all the women work in some fashion or another, some off the books so they can still collect various benefits from the government. Because the homeboys live at the pleasure of their wives' or girlfriends' mother or grandmother, and because many have no job and no prospects, they are low in the family pecking order—treated not so differently from the children. Not much is expected of them, either.

Until recently, the word *gang* wasn't used in connection with V-13. Gang was something the police called them, something the newspapers called them. To themselves, they were, and have always been, simply a *neighborhood*: people who live in a place where they've lived all their lives, where their parents have lived all *their* lives. To the Chicanos of Oakwood, this one square mile is their village, their home, their world, a society within society. Everyone knows everyone, and they have known each other since they were born. When somebody disrespects the neighborhood—when somebody from Culver City hits Lutie's mom on the head with a bumper jack, or takes a knife to Beaver, or a bat to Tavo, or shoots Gato in the back—the neighborhood is supposed to make sure somebody from Culver City is bumper-jacked or knifed or clubbed or shot. It is the job of the men to protect the honor of the neighborhood. This is the meaning of the expression "down for the hood." Either you is or you ain't.

Lately the youngbloods of V-13 have been eatin' cheese. Three times over the past ten days, gang members from Culver City, Chicanos from the projects in the town next door to Venice, have driven through the neighborhood and taken potshots at Venice people. Unfortunately, Yogi and Lil' Sleeper and the rest have been too fucked up on crack to continue their four-generation cycle of violence. Even the social workers have begun to notice.

"I remember the Venice from when I was gangbanging," says Marianne Diaz, 29, a former member of the Compadres, another Chicano gang in Los Angeles. She is now an outreach worker with Community Youth Gang Services.

"Venice is such a big, old gang," she says. "Even back in the day they had, like, maybe a thousand homeboys. They were down. People respected them. Venice, Lennox, and South Los, and Eighteenth Street. Those are your four big gangs. Everyone has heard of Venice. I mean, if you got busted, you were gonna see twenty or thirty of them down in the pen, and they were the ones running things. Just about every older Venice homeboy I meet is a *veterano*," an ex-con.

In Venice, she says, a high percentage of the males over fifteen have been to jail or to juvenile. "He figures the system is against him, that no one wants to give him a chance. And he also figures there's a good chance he will die tomorrow. It is a very live-for-today society." In his nineteen years, Lil' Sleeper has done a total of four years behind bars; Yogi is about to go off and serve a one-year sentence. He says he's innocent of the actual crime for which he was found guilty, but he's taking it like a man: "I figured I'd already done about thirty or forty *other* burglaries. They had to get me for one of them."

Being respected in the neighborhood for being an ex-con is only one aspect of a curious system of beliefs in Venice. Take the Gonzales family. On a typical Saturday night in the living room there is popcorn and a video, adults and kids. Three people in the room, of varying ages, are nodding out from heroin. A joint of *yeska* is being passed around. The daughter's boyfriend and two of his friends are bustling in and out from the back yard, smoking crack. At one point, Great-grandma looks up from the movie. "Oh, Sleeper, I *know* you are doing that shit again." She laughs heartily, setting her chins ajiggle. "You are sprunger than a motherfucker!" Everybody in the room guffaws.

Over the years, one homeboy's father, a $22,000-a-year city employee, has borrowed a total of $40,000 to bail out and defend his son for various crimes. Another's father took a week off from work to help his son kick his heroin habit. "I just love my boy," the father says. "What would you do?"

By the time gang members reach the age of twenty-five—if they live so long—they usually move toward a more settled life. Many work in city sanitation and maintenance. Delivery services are another good shot for ex-cons. Almost all of them have children; their culture puts a high value on the young; they want to see their *niños* grow up. War is a young man's game. The OGs rest on their laurels.

"The older homeboys are saying that the younger guys, all they care about is getting high," Diaz says. "They're telling them, 'You like to wear Venice on your hat, you like to write your name on the walls and throw up a hand sign and get tattoos all over your body, but you won't bust a grape on nobody.'"

Back in the 1940s and 1950s, says Diaz, the Chicano gangs that emerged in Southern California were "more or less derived from the Hispanic culture." Descendants of the Mexican *banditos*, and later of the zoot suiters, they inherited a macho culture dedicated to the preservation of territory and respect.

"Now," Diaz says, "things are changing. The rock cocaine has come in, and the Blacks have taken over the gang thing. My partner, who is Black, he always tell me, 'My people took your idea of gangs and totally bent it and turned it around and took away any of the pride or the respect.' I think that's true. It's like before, in the old days, the leader of a gang was the homeboy who was downest. Now it's the homeboy who is richest. In Venice, nobody's got nothing anymore. It's all about getting high."

***

Lil' Sleeper and Yogi are back in the room, both of them siting on the bed. It's morning. Or maybe it's afternoon. They've been smoking a few rocks.

"*Pssssst. Psssssssst!*"

Yogi starts. His eyes go wide. "What was that?" he whispers.

"What?" asks Lil' Sleeper. He looks up from the carpet, where he's been searching for crumbs.

"That noise," Yogi says. He turns down the radio, switches off the fan, cocks an ear.

"What noise?" Lil' Sleeper repeats.

"Hey, *Yogi!* Lemme in, *ese!*"

Yogi pulls back the curtain on the window over his bed. Outside there is daylight. The palms rustle in the breeze. Into the room waft the scents of salty sea, pink hydrangeas, refried beans, blue exhaust from souped-up cars. It is Panther. He holds up a dove, a twenty-dollar rock, about the size of a marble.

Yogi's bedroom is the unofficial clubhouse for the members of the Little Banditos, a twelve-member *cliqua* within the V-13 gang, which numbers roughly 300. A *cliqua* is an age-affinity group of homies who were all jumped into the gang at the same time—sort of like a pledge class in a fraternity. Like a soccer or basketball club, the Venice gang has a number of *cliquas* for different age groups, ranging from early teens to late twenties. There are the Banditos, the Little Banditos, the Tiny Banditos, the Midget Banditos. Likewise, within the gang, there are *cliquas* of Locos, Winos, Chucos, and Dukes, all of them with subgroups ranging from Midgets to Bigs.

Whenever the Little Banditos come by Yogi's crib, they follow the same procedure. They check first with Yogi at the window, then they go around to the front of the house and knock politely at the door. Permitted entrance, they exchange pleasantries in the front room—like so many brown-skinned Eddie Haskels, talkin' polite shit to Yogi's mom, his grandfather, and his little sister. Then they walk down the hallway to the back room, Yogi's crib. His mom thinks they're watching television and videos all day long. Or maybe she doesn't. Over the past month, since he got his tax-refund check (he worked for his uncle's landscaping company last summer), Yogi has not been away from his room for longer than an hour. The more crack you do, the harder it is to leave the pipe and sally forth.

"First hit!" Yogi calls, in the same manner he calls "shotgun" if you're driving him somewhere.

"It's *my* rock," Panther protests.

"Yeah, but it's my *room*." There is nothing worse than having a rock and nowhere to smoke it. You need somewhere cool and quiet. Somewhere nobody will bother you. If you don't pay attention, you can fuck off your high, which means you don't take advantage of the rush. It's only there for a little while. You can easily miss it. And then all you're left with is the jittery need for more.

Panther hands over the rock.

Yogi slices it with a razor blade, puts a piece the size of a small aquarium stone into his car-antenna-pipe. He melts it some with a Bic lighter, blows out all the air in his lungs, takes a blast. You can't hit it too hard or the hit will liquefy, and you'll lose it; later you'll have to scrape it out of the pipe. The resin is like the mint after dessert.

As soon as Yogi finishes his hit, Lil' Sleeper snatches the pipe from his hand; he and Panther begin to argue over who's next.

Yogi sits back and closes his eyes. Finally, he exhales—a light, clean smoke that smells of ether. Upon his next intake of fresh air, there is a supercharge effect—an instant explosion of pleasure inside his head, an orgasmic body rush. It drills a hole from the top of his scalp down to his groin, and then it drills another between his ears—an ecstatic, physical, electric sign of the cross. The music from the radio comes flooding into his head. His brain buzzes. He smiles cherubically, eyes slightly crossed.

Then the smile recedes, the feeling starts to fade. He begins thinking about the next hit.

One more hit.

More.

That's *all* he can think about. All he cares about.

His teeth clench, his jaw muscles stand, his throat tightens. Everything inside tightens. His veins constrict, his dick shrivels, his heart pounds. He lights another cigarette.

With each subsequent hit, the rush is less intense, but the desire for the next hit becomes *more* intense. With heroin, you have a twice-a-day obligation. You fix the morning and night and forget about it. Crack is different. It's moment to moment. You do a hit, feel the rush, start obsessing immediately about the next hit. About getting more. And more. One more hit. If you can stop yourself from thinking about it for thirty minutes, the urge will pass. You'd be jittery and speedy, but you can ride it out.

But you can't *not* think about it. Your every thought is focused on the next hit.

And the next hit is never as good.

You don't care.

You keep going.

You are *sprung*.

***

"So what are we gonna do?" Yogi asks. He is sitting on the bed in his narrow room. It is noon on another day. The drugs are gone, again. Lil' Sleeper is here, as usual. Panther is out trying to get some money some *vato* owes him.

"Let's go get a rock," Lil' Sleeper says, as if it's a new idea.

"You got any *fedia?*"

"No."

"You do *so*."

"I do not."

"Don't bullshit me, *ese*."

The way you find rock in the neighborhood is this: You walk outside of your house.

Day or night, rock is always for sale. You can buy it from men or women, boys or girls. You can buy it on corners, in alleys, through windows, inside apartment buildings. The dealers here don't even bother with packaging—no glassine envelopes, no vials. They sell the *pedasos* loose. The rocks are hard, white, crystalline, irregular. Cooked down from powder cocaine, using baking soda to trigger the chemical changes, they are pure and insoluble. The dealers stash the *pedasos* in their socks, in baggies, in pockets, beneath their tongues— a place the cops haven't yet learned to look; it won't be long. In the coming years, to frustrate the chain-of-custody considerations of the law, a more elaborate sales system will have to be developed: one guy to take the money, one guy to monitor a stash nobody physically possesses, an underage kid to deliver the actual rock. For now, though, things are simple. The dealer has the rocks. He works the curb. He *slings*.

There is constant commerce. There are businesslike slickers with theme raps ("I'm Billy D./Stick with me"). There are hot babes, cold gangstas, skinny rock dawgs—by five in the morning, they are scrapping and arguing like extras from the set of *Night of the Living Dead*, trying to sell another rock to go score more. Besides the members of V-13 and their families—one night I partied with a group of women in their thirties and forties, all of whom were gainfully employed; they smoked *way* more crack than the homies could ever even afford—the customers are a steady stream of *gavachos*, White people in nice cars, residents of nearby Marina Del Ray, Santa Monica, and Beverly Hills. The dealers rush aggressively into the street, surrounding the cars, sticking their hands inside, jockeying and fending for position ... vibrating, clenching, exhorting, "Take mine!" "Me!" "I got you!"

Most of the dealers are *miatas*, derogatory Chicano slang for African American—in this case members of the Shoreline Crips, whose families have coexisted with the Chicanos in Oakwood for years. Lately, there has been peace between the two gangs. The Shorelines have no beef with the *vatos* smoking up all the product they can sell.

Sleeper remembers the days when things were different.

"Nineteen seventy-seven was the first I remember somebody getting killed that I actually knew," he says. "And then, *bang*, all of a sudden there were like ten shootings a week. Homies were dropping left and right on both sides. It was all-out war. When we walked down the street, we carried a gun. We wore the whole outfit, the khakis and the Pendletons, the hairnets, the bandannas, the hats, the overcoats, the whole bit. We was clean, five creases in every shirt, and we ironed them ourselves. Between me, my brother, and my father, we used to go through two cans of spray starch a week.

"I sometimes carried a twelve-gauge shotgun under my overcoat. It was like the Wild West, man. You'd have homeboys on the roof, homeboys behind the trees, guns everywhere. For a while, when the National Guard had the streets barricaded, you could only get in by police escort. If a house got burned, the fire department wouldn't go in until sunrise. It was up to you to put it out. We was down, homeboy, wasn't nobody meaner."

In 1979, the media discovered the gang problem by the sea. The *Los Angeles Times* published its special report—an entire section. There were stories of stray bullets, innocent victims, grieving mothers, shattered lives, midnight death.

"THE TROUBLE IN OAKWOOD," read a subhead on the front page. "Swept by smog-free ocean breezes, bordered on the south by the affluent playground called Marina del Ray," the text read, "Oakwood is a strangely incongruous center of poverty and tragedy. While crime and gang violence tear at the community from within, mounting coastal real-estate values threaten to crush it from without."

At that time, the drugs of choice in the neighborhood were *chiva* and PCP. *Chiva* is Mexican slang for "goat." In this case, it's also slang for black tar heroin imported from Mexico. When *chiva* was the thing, the Chicanos ruled the L.A. drug trade. They had the cars and the money and the guns. They sold the heroin to the *miatas* and reaped the profits.

Since crack came to the hood, the *miatas* have been in control. The struggle to stay high is a difficult job. The homeboys beg their mothers or their wives or girlfriends for five or ten dollars. They say they have to get a new driver's license, or they find some other official-sounding excuse. They say they need a new asthma inhaler or another small, expensive thing that they can rip off from a drug store and produce later to back up their story. Scam done, they buy a couple hits and smoke. Then they start all over again, scamming to get more. Many have sold their tools and their father's tools. There are amazing deals floating around Venice at three in the morning— whole automotive tune-up kits for under fifty dollars, VCRs for twenty-five.

Many in Venice have also sold their guns, which is probably another reason the Venice homeboys have been unable to muster the manpower to pay back Culver City. Lil' Sleeper, for one, sold his shotgun about a month ago. One night, someone offered me a .22-caliber semiautomatic Ruger rifle for the price of a twenty-dollar rock. Absent something of value to sell, the homeboys will do a robbery or burglary, though when you're sprung, that sort of business takes way too long. And then there's the business of fencing the goods—gratification too long delayed.

"The worst thing," says Joe Alarcon, a former Lennox gang member who now works for Youth Gang Services, "is that at this point we don't have much to offer Venice. The problems are even bigger in South Central. Down there we're getting, like, five homicides a week. The Black areas are really bad. On a daily basis, something like 85 to 90 percent of all crimes in Los Angeles are being committed by Bloods and Crips. Those guys are crazy; they just don't care. Because our resources are limited, we've had to concentrate on the areas that are the worst. We've kind of let Venice fall through the cracks, I'm afraid."

***

Another day in Yogi's room. Yogi, Lil' Sleeper, and Margarita are on the bed.

Lil' Sleeper: "How much *fedia* you got?"

Yogi: "Two dollars, homes."

"I got two, too," says Lil' Sleeper. Really, he has five. He turns to Margarita. "You got *fedia?*"

Margarita's eyes are large, brown, empty. She looks like a beautiful, underage zombie model. One at a time, she works three crumpled dollar bills out of the front pocket of her super-tight denim miniskirt. Finished at last, she holds the bills aloft like a prize.

"That's six," Lil' Sleeper announces. He snatches the bills from her hand.

"Seven," Yogi contradicts.

"Wha'?"

"Two and two plus three equals *seven.*"

And then: A series of hard knocks on the door—*bang bang bang.*

Everybody ramrods. Eyes like saucers. *What the fuck, ese?*

Yogi turns down the radio and the fan. He calls out, innocently, musically: "Who's theeeeere?"

"Me, motherfucker! Open up!"

Yogi and Margarita trade looks. Lil' Sleeper's eyes bulge. He looks like he's about to throw up.

Five years ago, when Lil' Sleeper was still known as David and was about to be jumped into the gang, he went to Sleeper and asked him could he have his name. It is a common tradition, like adoption in reverse. Sleeper was honored. And he was willing. But there was a problem—another homeboy was *already* calling himself Lil' Sleeper. The thing was, *that* Lil' Sleeper had turned out to be a cheese eater. Sleeper was sorry he'd ever said yes to that *vato*. So, he said, if David wanted the handle for himself, Sleeper told him, he could have it. All he had to do was beat up the other Lil' Sleeper and take the name away.

The fight was bloody but short. David became Lil' Sleeper. Thereafter, he owed his allegiance to Sleeper.

Now Lil' Sleeper chews on his thumb, trying to think. "Open the door," he says at last.

Sleeper is hype. And he's even more pissed for being made to wait outside Yogi's bedroom door like some, like some ... *What the fuck, ese?* His jaw is clenched. The veins in his neck are tight. He points a dirty calloused finger at his namesake.

"What have you done to pay back Culver City?" he demands.

Lil' Sleeper looks up at him defiantly. "We ain't gonna do *nothing*," he says.

"We ain't gonna do *nothing*," Yogi repeats. He's got his homey's back. Little Banditos 4-ever.

"You got shot at the other day in your own neighborhood, homeboy! You got shot at *three times* in one week!"

Lil' Sleeper shrugs. "Why's it up to *me* to do something? There's other people who live here, too."

Sleeper stares at him in disbelief. *Can you believe this punk?* Then his eyes drift down to the carpet. There are lots of little white pieces of paper and lint and cloth and cigarette ash down there. To him, each piece looks like a rock. Could be a rock. He wants to reach down and ...

"Gimme a blast," Sleeper demands. His lips are pulled back in a tight grimace.

"We was just going to get a ten from Binky," Yogi says.

"A ten?" Sleeper chews his thumb, considering.

Yogi brightens. "Maybe we could get him to kick us down a little more."

"Hand me that pipe," Sleeper says. "Is there any residue in there?"

"What about Culver City?" asks Margarita.

"We'll get them later," Sleeper says.

FACT:
FIVE OUT OF FIVE KIDS WHO KILL LOVE SLAYER

Kids who listen to Slayer are "violent and heavy drug users," says one expert. "The band members worship Satan," says another. All of which has had a predictable effect on the band's popularity. Perception meets reality.

In red smoke and chaos the demon appears, a spirit in black leather before a field of broken skulls and empty coffins, eyes gleaming, maniacal grin, hair a nimbus of floodlit hellfire. Sweat drips down his tattooed arm, splashes his bass guitar. He steps to the microphone, hocks a fat loogie center stage. The spots click green. He roars:

"*Are you ready to diiiiiiiiiiiiiiie!?*"

A scream erupts, pandemonium, the primal cheer of six thousand lost young souls from the Heartland, the ticket holders who lined up five hours before showtime to see a concert that wasn't even advertised. (Why bother? None of them read a paper or listen to radio.) Ripped jeans and pimples, bustiers and black spandex minis, cigarettes dangling beneath peach fuzz, metal crosses kissing sweaty virgin skin, mall rats and jailbait and bedroom air guitarists, they are America's future, the fans of a thrash-metal band called Slayer, jammed now, pelvis to buttock, into this civic arena on a full-moon Sabbath eve to take dark communion at the headbangers ball.

The band explodes, a crunching engagement of chain-saw guitars, gutshot bass, thumping drums, feedback thundering from amp stacks two stories high. The drummer beats from a platform in the rafters. Stage left, the rhythm guitarist wears a forearm sheath bristling with tenpenny nails. Stage right, the lead guitarist glares, rakes the strings. There's a hole in the crotch of his leather pants. The demon on the bass bangs his head against the air, furious, down and up, down and up, then switches to figure eights, pounding to the beat of the drum, throwing sweat and musk from his thick, wavy mane. He rolls his eyes back into his head. The spots click red. He sings, hoarse and throaty:

Propaganda death ensemble
Burial to be
Corpses rotting through the night
In blood-laced misery
Scorched earth the policy
The reason for the siege
The pendulum it shaves the blade
The strafing air blood raid

Beneath the stage, just past a buffer manned by bouncers, kids are crammed and jammed and smashed behind a chest-high wooden barricade. Elbows in windpipes, noses in armpits, ears ringing, hearts pounding, heads banging down and up, synapses frying endorphins and kilowatts, bathtub acid and homicidal dreams, fists thrusting toward the stage, index and pinkie fingers extended like horns, the sign of the master of darkness, Hail Satan!

The air hums and buzzes, and in the middle of the floor of this vast, round, seatless auditorium, the mosh pit begins to swarm. Shirtless boys and fearless girls—fourteen, sixteen, twenty years old, braces, tattoos, Charlie perfume, half-shaved heads—skip aggressively counterclockwise, cherubs in the inferno, gathering speed, shoulders cocked, elbows crooked like linemen, grinning, grimacing, laughing, crying, bouncing, and ricocheting like agitated electrons, like pinballs trapped between bonus bumpers. Here and there one is borne aloft, passed toward the stage on a sea of palms, kicking and screaming and rolling back to front, dumped headfirst over the barricade, to be carried away by a bouncer.

Infiltration push reserves
Encircle the front lines
Supreme art of strategy
Playing on the minds
Bombard till submission

Take all to their graves
Indication of triumph
The number that are dead

Away from the mayhem, all along the perimeter of the arena, every fire door and exit is guarded by a rent-a-cop and two parents with flashlights. They patrol the grim scene with fearful eyes. Outside, near the entrance, a group of Teens for Christ urges leaflets and brimstone upon dopers and metalheads straggling late into the show. Later, two city cops on mountain bikes will ride up hard and adrenalized on a circle of autograph hounds, looking to make a bust. This is Sacramento, California, but it could be any town that Slayer has seen over the ten-week, forty-seven-date cross-country tour called Seasons in the Abyss.

As usual, the sight on the horizon of the four horsemen of Slayer had been cause for panic in cities like Tucson, Milwaukee, Grand Rapids, Poughkeepsie. Newspapers ran foreboding headlines: SLAYER: THEY'RE FROM THE BLOOD, DEATH, BEELZEBUB CAMP. WITH DEADLY LYRICS, SLAYER STALKS FANS. Insurance costs were quoted, editorials were written, past incidents were cited. In New York, fans tore out seat cushions and sailed them onstage. In Philadelphia, they pulled down the sprinkler system and flooded the hall. In Hollywood, tickets sold out and two hundred thrashers rioted; one of them is charged with trying to run over a cop with his van.

Everywhere Slayer went, city fathers and mothers slapped palms to foreheads, My Lord, what now? Since the plagues of AIDS and crack had risen up to smite the Me Decade, America had been tripping on guilt. Penitent, confused, afraid, people joined groups and clubs. They started going to church, reciting the pledge, curbing their appetites. They became religious fundamentalists, Meese commissioners, new conservatives, L. Ron Hubbarders, self-helpers, liquid dieters, right-to-lifers. Hollering warnings, they laid their bodies across every alternative exit on the highway of life, trying to detour choice. Reins were tightened. "Do your own thing" was scrapped for "Just say no." Control. Control. Control. That was the answer. Be a community watchdog. Join a health club. Accept the Lord. Eat yogurt instead of ice cream. Drink bubbles instead of beer. Wear a condom, close your eyes, never question authority.

At least that's what grown-up America was thinking. The kids, meanwhile, were in their own world, listening to another kind of music. Heavy metal, speed metal, death metal, thrash, its focus was devil fantasy, the occult, death, destruction, doom. The groups they idolized had names like Black Sabbath, Metallica, Anthrax, Suicidal Tendencies, Megadeth. Perverse, contrary, heavy metal was a new soundtrack of protest, a reaction against the reactionaries, a cracked mirror in the haunted house of the modern age. Parents began finding notebooks doodled with pentagrams. They barged through bedroom doors, stood horrified as the stereo blared and little Johnny banged his head against the air.

Soon, lawmakers and experts began their own counterassault. A group of political wives led the way, decrying heavy metal for "exposing innocent children to themes of sadomasochism, rape, and suicide." A group called Back in Control demanded a ban on heavy metal concerts and said children who listen to thrash should be "depunked and demetaled before it's too late." William F. Buckley Jr. called for censorship.

Kids who listen to Slayer, said a Los Angeles psychologist, "are violent and heavy drug users, they have no positive orientation." Said a Tennessee psychologist: "The lyrics become their philosophy." An eighteen-year-old boy shoots himself in the head while heavy metal blasts from his car stereo. A fourteen-year-old girl stabs and then bludgeons her mother to death. Seven teens ransack a warehouse, paint SUICIDAL DEATH TRIBE on the wall, jam a dead rat through the plaster. A teenager pleads guilty to mutilating cats and using the blood to scrawl 666 on elementary school walls. Each of the five panel members on a Phil Donahue show titled "Kids Who Kill" name Slayer as their favorite band.

All of which has had a predictable effect on Slayer's popularity. Ten years ago they were playing in high school gyms. Five years ago they were on the road in a rental van and a Camaro. In 1990 the band's sixth album, *Seasons in the Abyss*, made *Billboard* magazine's Top

40 pop chart. In July of that year, Slayer came of age: The cover of *Rolling Stone*.

> *Sport the war, war support*
> *The sport is total war*
> *When victory's a massacre*
> *When victory is survival*
> *When the end is a slaughter*
> *The final swing is not a drill*
> *It's how many people I can kill*

Back in Sacramento, with "War Ensemble" nearing its final, deafening chords, a young thrasher pushes his way through the crowd, bouncing off bodies like a drunk sailor tacking through a blow. His eyes are bloodshot, one shoe is missing, his hair is matted to his pink forehead. His brand-new Slayer concert T-shirt, black with a yellow death head ($22), is shredded. He reaches the cinder-block wall, leans there a moment, dazed.

He stares upward, focusing vaguely on the ceiling, the stroboscopic colored lights, the smoke, the din. What's running through his mind? Maybe a photomontage, quick cuts like MTV, images collected in his brain. A soldier's arms shot away. Cops beating a man with batons. A psycho slicing skin from the back of an attractive blond corpse. An electric chair. A mushroom cloud. A Patriot missile. Burning crude. George Bush. Steven Seagal. Undercover narcs breaking down a door in a ghetto. Kurds rioting for food. A cow bloating in a rice paddy. Protesters smashing windows. Al Sharpton. Elvis. Christina Applegate. Freddy Krueger. A demon thrashing in a fiery quagmire. Whitney Houston singing "The Star-Spangled Banner."

Suddenly, the kid stirs. His brows rise, his mouth contorts, his eyes blaze. He screams loud, long piercing ...

"*Ahhhhhhhhhhhhhhhh!*"

Then he slams his head, once, hard, into the cinder-block wall.

"Killer, dude!" he says.

"Check this one out, dude," says Tom Araya, waving a piece of fan mail. He sets down the letter, takes a hit off a bong he rigged from a Bart Simpson drinking bottle, free from 7-Eleven when you buy a Big Gulp.

Tom is the demon on the bass, Slayer's leader, home now from the road, catching up on his mail. He sits cross-legged on the sand-colored carpet in his newly acquired stucco rambler, white with baby-blue trim, the same color as his '85 Camaro. The house sits amid the vast sprawling suburbs of the San Fernando Valley. This exit off the 210 Freeway is Santa Anita, the town is Arcadia, though it really could be any exit on this grid-planned, fertile plain of mini-malls, stoplights, palm trees, video outlets, frozen-yogurt stores, everything stucco—beige, tan, or cream.

Tom's piece of the lifestyle cost him two and a quarter. It's his first purchase, he's proud of it. Real estate is, like, real, you know? But it also makes him nervous. The payments. Being a Top 40 thrash idol grossed Tom only $90,000 in 1990. He's going to have to wait awhile before buying furniture. For now he's making do with the stuff from his old room at his parents' house. The decor is Early Teenage Suburbanoid, a kind of three-bedroom bedroom—Adults Beware! His pride is his video workshop: a chair, a desk, two monitors, two VCRs. His hobby is homemade music videos. He makes them using Slayer songs and scenes from movies like *Henry, Portrait of a Serial Killer, Platoon,* and *Scarface.* He likes mutilation clips, soldiers, and sexy girls best.

Tom's hair is in a ponytail that stretches midway down his back. On his index finger is a white-gold skull with two ruby eyes, $800, custom-made at a franchise jewelry store in the mall. A little gold ornament dangles from his right ear, some kind of Hebrew blessing, half of it anyway. The other half dangles from the ear of his ex-girlfriend, Teri, guitarist in a metal band called Harum Scarum. They were together three years. Recently they called it quits, which, incidentally, was the name of a disco band that Tom once played in—Quits.

Anyway, Tom's alone now, sort of. There's this one girl begging him to come to Oakland. And another from Dallas who's ready to miss classes and fly out at her own expense. But the one he really likes lives in New Jersey. He doesn't know whether to call her or not. He's always the one who calls. Why is it that when you show someone you like her, she runs the other way? Why don't you get the ones you really want?

Those, of course, are questions with no answer, questions put out of mind right now as Tom exhales his fragrant sinsemilla bong hit and reads a letter. This fan, like Tom, like all four members of Slayer, grew up a little south of here. Tom was born in Chile, moved with his family to Huntington Park, California, when he was five years old. His voice is soft and lilting, a mixture of Valley doper, Teenage Mutant Ninja Turtle, and mambo king.

"Sittin' in the desert, jammin' to 'South of Heaven,' where I'm sixty miles from where the fun will begin. My favorite tune is 'Expendable Youth.' With our jobs and what we do, that's all we actually are. I also like 'Angel of Death' and 'Mandatory Suicide.' I think of that song when I'm firing my Echo 3 M-60 machine gun. Being a grunt is pure motivation—like your music. It puts me in the right state of mind for war. You can count on four dead Iraqis for you guys. Keep kickin' ass, dudes!"

"Cool, huh?" says Tom, giggling. During Desert Storm, 20 percent of Slayer's fan mail came from soldiers.

Tom is twenty-nine, boyish, endearing, handsome in a roguish sort of way, with a good hit of Indian in his cheekbones and light skin like his mother, a lay minister in the Catholic church, a hairdresser who wears her Slayer jacket to work. When she opened her own beauty shop, Tom and his six brothers and sisters tried to think up a cool name. They suggested the Harem or the Tease, but in the end she settled on her own choice, Cinderella.

"Whoa! Listen to this!" Tom exclaims. He flops down, elbow to carpet, palm to ear, legs stretched out with his shoes off. He reads:

"What's up? I am one of your most devoted fucking fans. You guys are gods in my eyes, I mean, fuck, I'm fucking obsessed with you guys. I'm a hardcore Satanist and I'm also into black magic. I read Tom's interview in the *L.A. Times*, and I don't believe you're a Catholic, I hope you were lying your ass off. I'm fifteen and your music is the only thing that has kept me from losing my mind. Most people go mad with anger and want to go out and kill someone after listening to Slayer. Not me. It soothes my brain."

Tom picks up his Bart pipe, loads a bud, a gift from a fan in Sacramento. The deader the town, it seems, the better the bud. Tom wonders if there's a correlation. He surveys the room, fires up the bowl. He was supposed to paint the living room today, but it's raining, he feels lazy. Maybe tomorrow. He picks up another letter.

"Your music takes me away to a far-off plain, where lies a faithless depth and Hades rapes in clouds. Tom, man, you're really cool. When you sing songs where you hit high notes, it gets me really hyper and glad I'm a headbanger." Two girls from Finland write: "A few days ago we bought Metal Hammer's poster book. There was a picture of you. Tom's balls were so grand (big dick, huge genital, massive gun, sharp sword, manly bar)."

Tom shakes his head and laughs. "This shit scares me sometimes," he says. "The way kids are into us, the way the adults hate us. *Nobody* gets it. It's amazing. Shit, dude! It's all right off TV."

Take "Mandatory Suicide." It's a song about being a soldier, about the draft. Substitute suicide for draft, he says. But it's not antiauthority. It's about informed choice. If you're going to join the army, then know that some general may possibly order your death. That's the duty of a soldier. "And thinking about death," Tom says, "I was wondering what it would be like to get shot. I've seen a lot of people shot in the movies, and I've had dreams where I was shot, so I have an idea, I know that it would burn like hell. I don't think the pain would be as bad as the burning sensation would be."

"Hallowed Point" is about owning guns. If you're gonna have one, it says, be prepared to make a hallowed point. Hallowed point comes from hollow point, as in the kind of bullet. Tom's not against guns. He's thinking of getting one. "Shooting somebody's a lot better than getting your head bashed in," he says.

"Blood Red" was inspired by news footage of a Chinese student playing cat and mouse with a tank in Tiananmen Square. "I read these little news clips about how things are fucked up here, fucked up there, everybody's got a civil war. And the way it goes down, the new guys are just as bad as the old," he says. "Dead Skin Mask" was inspired by mass murderer Ed Gein. "I can't tell you why I'm fascinated with mass murderers," Tom says. "It's like, there are actually all these people out there whose world is murder. They have to pretend to survive in this world with everybody else, but really they're living this hell. That really trips me out."

Tom wrote "War Ensemble" months before Iraq invaded Kuwait. It's not that he was prescient. It's just that he's fascinated with war, or anyway, with movies about war: *Full Metal Jacket, Apocalypse Now, Hamburger Hill.* To write the lyrics he consulted a military textbook.

"Living in the times we do," Tom says, "you don't *have* to make anything up. You got to admit, what goes on in the world is pretty fuckin' bizarre."

Tom pauses a moment, considering his words, reaching into the baggie. He loads another bud into the Bart bong. He's proud of his pipe. With all the head shops gone, a good bong is hard to come by, even though it's pretty easy to get drugs. He flicks his Bic, covers the rush hole he bored with his Swiss Army knife, moves the flame slowly toward the bowl, a salvaged piece from a very old pipe. He draws at the convenient plastic straw built into the top of the bottle, making the sound of bubbles.

Mid-hit, he freezes. He tilts his head, listens. "Shit!" he exclaims. "Light a cigarette!"

Tom jumps up from the floor, grabs the Bart bong, the baggie, the papers, a few loose joints. He scrams into the bedroom.

A knock at the door. A pause. A key.

The door opens. In steps Dad. He looks around, sniffs. Behind him, side by side, are John and Ollie. Tom's younger brother and sister are one year apart, inseparable.

"The whole house smells like pot!" says Dad.

Ollie raises an eyebrow. John smirks.

Dad strolls toward Tom's bedroom. Ollie and John follow.

"Oh! Hey, Dad!" says Tom, backing out of his closet.

Dad regards his son a moment. He frowns, shakes his head. "I thought you said you were painting today."

"Mommy, I like that one!" croons the little boy. He's wearing surf shorts and mirrored goggles on a sunny, big-sky day near Phoenix. "The white one, Mom!"

Another subdivision, six hours east on the 10 Freeway, the same minimalls and yogurt stores, but here the boulevards are wider, the stucco and neon set back from the road, sheep and horses grazing on backyard farms. It's the hometown of the Greenway High School Devils, the Desert Hills Evangelical Free Church, and Kerry King, Slayer's rhythm guitarist.

"I'll tell you," says Kerry, walking over to a white puppy turning excited circles in the last stall of the kennel. "If you're interested in this girl, you should get into showing."

"What does that consist of?" asks Mom, who has yet to convince Dad that the kids need a $1,500 pet. This is her umpteenth visit, but Kerry doesn't mind. He had to feed everybody anyway—twenty Akita sires and bitches and pups, some homebred, some from Illinois, a championship line. "Do you have to take them out of state?"

"The big guns do," says Kerry. "Like, I'm getting into the big-gun area myself."

"Do you show them?"

"I do, ah, I don't. I mean, I don't really have the look," says Kerry, the one who wears the sheath with the tenpenny nails onstage. "You've got to have a more contemporary look. I have a handler who shows them."

"Wouldn't that be discrimination?" asks Mom. "I mean, if your dog is—"

"You know how the world is, ma'am," says Kerry. "People have weird ideas."

Kerry's been living in Phoenix now for about eighteen months. He came here because he needed room to raise his dogs, chickens, and rats, the latter to feed his snakes. He has a collection of two hundred serpents, mostly boas. He also collects vintage Corvettes, horror videos, Slayer memorabilia, sports memorabilia. Kerry has always been a collector. You could say he collected Slayer.

It began in 1981, when he was fourteen. He and Jeff Hanneman met one day when both showed up to audition for a guitar slot in a band. Several days later, Dave Lombardo, a drummer, introduced himself when he was delivering a pizza to Kerry's neighborhood. He'd heard about the spoiled kid in the corner house with the collection of vintage guitars. Kerry was little and skinny then, pretty surfed out for someone who lived so far from the beach. His father was an aircraft-parts inspector who used to pluck "Red River Valley" on an acoustic. The Kings lived in a Mexican neighborhood; Kerry spent his youth running from *cholos*. After being caught and beaten a few times, he was forbidden by his parents to leave the backyard.

Having collected two guitarists and a drummer, Kerry called Tom for bass and vocals. Tom was working evenings as a respiratory therapist and was back in school to become a nurse. The four convened in Tom's garage. They jammed. Things clicked. They got themselves a manager, a friend trying to break into that side of the business.

And so a band was born. They called it Slayer, you know, like a murderer. Cool. They stole wood from construction sites and hammered together a drum riser and two guitar platforms, made a light frame with floods stolen from a high school gym and put on their first show. Tom's little brother, John, was the only roadie. He worked the lights and sound, and when a guitar string broke he'd run backstage and fix it. Soon they were on the road up and down the West Coast. Tom, the only member over twenty-one, was in charge. The towns had names like Winnipeg, and the crowds were small, but the boys were living their dream, playing in a rock 'n' roll band.

In 1983, Tom and Kerry's father put up $3,000 to cut an album. *Show No Mercy* sold sixty thousand copies, staggering for a band that nobody had heard of. The *Los Angeles Times* would later say that it "codified the gruesome conventions of death metal and became one of the most imitated albums ever made."

The rest, as they say, is show-biz history. More albums, harder lyrics, higher sales for records titled *Hell Awaits, Reign in Blood, South of Heaven, Seasons in the Abyss, Decade of Aggression.*

Mom and her kids are gone, and Kerry is reclining on a patio chaise in his living room. Behind him, on a shelf, is a huge softball trophy. Kerry sponsored the championship team, the Vipers, for two seasons, played third base. Last season, he had to be away on Slayer's European tour, so he decided not to sponsor it again, though he did pay his fee to remain on the roster. He showed up at the fourth game. After warm-ups, Kerry went to take a leak. The team took the field. They never did let him play.

Kerry writes most of Slayer's devil songs: "Skeletons of Society," "Born of Fire," "Temptation." He is about to recite one called "Spirit in Black." In the corner of the room, a trophy of another land, an exotic dancer from Denver, peddles an exercycle. He recites deadpan from the lyric sheet that comes with the *Seasons* CD, looking up now and again for effect:

> *Welcome to my world*
> *Involve yourself within my dream*
> *Experience a life*
> *Just like your mind thought not to be*
> *Take a look through time*
> *At past or present worlds to be*
>
> *I rule this inferno*
> *Enthroned for eternity*
> *Spirits damned to rot*
> *Amidst the brimstone fireballs*
> *Eyes of the dead*
> *Watching from their living walls*
>
> *Broken-glass reflections*
> *Show your flesh eaten away*
> *Listen closely to my voice*
> *Feed me all your hatred*
> *Empty all your thoughts to me*
> *I can fill your emptiness*
> *With immortality*

"That one, hmmmm, let me see," says Kerry, tilting his head professionally, one finger to his lip. "Oh, yeah. I was at Blockbuster Video, and there was a video called ... something about hell. It completely inspired me to write this song about a hell-like world and somebody being in charge of it. It's a fictitious story. It's like, welcome to my fantasy. Everybody would like to have his own world. Like, when you're in my place, you're in my rules, my boundaries, I can make anything happen that I want, 'cause it's my place. I'm the authority. Kind of like a man's home is his castle sort of thing.

"It's like, I try to write songs that are very visual. You can read the lyrics and see what's going on. Like that line, 'Eyes of the dead watching from their living halls.' I got that from *The Sword and the Sorcerer*, that part in the movie where they're conjuring up that guy, and he rises out of this casket of blood and there's this wall of faces, and once he comes to life all the faces come to life.

"That's where I get a lot of my images, from movies. And also stuff I imagine in my mind. Like in 'Spirit,' the first two verses sort of build you a picture of the place. 'Spirits damned to rot,' 'Broken-glass reflections'—you know, you're looking at yourself in a broken mirror or something. It's all visuals, things that are spooky, cool, stuff like that. See, if I had a choice to go to any kind of movie, it would be a horror movie. It's like, *Nightmare on Elm Street*. When that came out, it was just so unique, so well done, I was like, Oh, man, this, like, changes my whole life. *Friday the 13th*, *The First Power*, *Leviathan*, *Night Breed*. All those are really killer movies.

"I describe my songs as horror movies on music," he says. "It's a fantasy world. Tom likes war, serial killers, current-events stuff like that. But I don't know where people get this idea that I worship Satan. I'm not a satanic guy."

Late afternoon in the High Sierras. The land is flat; a snow-capped mountain rises in the distance. Two hours northeast of Los Angeles, the suburbs continue their migration toward the desert and Barstow, a new exit off the freeway, a new development of identical stuccos right next to a new mall. In a cul-de-sac, a family of Asians—Mom,

Dad, two kids—stands at the edge of their new cement sidewalk, peering hopefully into manicured dirt, looking for signs of lawn.

"How y'all?!" yells Dave Lombardo, waving from across the street. He pulls a box out of the trunk of his car, a jacked-up Pontiac with a supercharger poked through the hood. "They got a housing committee out here," Dave whispers. "They like you to be friendly."

Dave and Theresa Lombardo have just moved into their first house, an upscale number with a vaulted foyer and neo-Victorian half-moon windows in the front, an expanse of dirt yard enclosed by nine-foot cinder-block walls in back. Dave heads up the sidewalk, checking for signs of his own lawn. He removes his shoes, backs through the front door, pads over the runner on the new white carpet.

"Where do you want this?" he hollers.

Theresa appears at the top of the stairs, floral stretch pants and big hair. She puts her finger to her lips.

"Don't shout!" she whispers. "You'll make the cake fall. Put that stuff in the kitchen. Tiptoe!"

Dave smiles, tiptoes, putting down the box, moving into the living room, where he begins alphabetizing his CD collection across the fireplace mantel. Theresa comes downstairs. They kiss. She goes to the powder room, busies herself arranging a new set of matching mauve bath accessories. She hums.

Dave and Theresa are at their best when they're together, and they're always together, kind of like Barbie and Ken, which is what the other members of Slayer have nicknamed them. During the hours before a concert, while the rest of the band sleeps, Dave and Theresa usually play tourist. In Sacramento they saw the Governor's Mansion, Dave in his long hair and Slayer cap, Theresa in her stretch pants, bobby socks, spike heels, and pancake makeup. As a souvenir they bought a magnet for the new fridge.

At the concerts, Theresa waits at the bottom of Dave's two-story platform. He plays a console of twelve custom-made drums and eight extra-thick cymbals, the largest of which he got because it makes the sound of two trucks colliding. His earliest memories of drums are Tarzan movies and Santería ceremonies. His parents, who are from

Havana, used to bring him. He played along on toy bongos. Now he has his very own roadie and a set worth $15,000.

When Dave plays, high above the crowd, chills run up and down his spine, he gets goosebumps. It's incredible, he's not good with words, but it's an incredible feeling, the energy, the electricity between him and the kids, it just blows him away. Used to be Slayer was playing and Dave would be watching the kids go crazy, watching them fly all over the room, and it looked like so much fun that he couldn't just sit there on his stool. He'd be like, "I'm gonna jump in too," and he'd climb down off his platform and dive right into the crowd. He'd free fall, and the kids would catch him, and then they'd just, like, hold him up, just, like, floating around, and then they'd throw him back onstage.

It was fun. He did it every show. Then kids started stealing his shoes, ripping his shirt, pulling out locks of hair. Then one night he got punched in the face by a bouncer. Never again, dude.

Now when he's finished, Theresa bundles him up in a robe and takes him around the waist, leads him to the showers. They started dating years ago, while she was a bookkeeper at Sears and he was a security guard at Kmart. These days, they don't really mix much with the band. Dave quit a while back because the guys gave Theresa so much shit, locker-room antics, dick jokes and such. He's back now because after he left, the band never got around to auditioning a new drummer.

Even with the hassles, Dave is thrilled to be in Slayer. Thanks to tours, he and Theresa have seen castles in Scotland, beer factories in Germany, the Imperial Gardens in Japan, a big, humongous church in Milano. They try to make the most of things as they are right now. They don't know how long stardom is gonna last. Nothing lasts forever. (Within nine months, in fact, Dave and Theresa would split up.)

"It's still an incredible thing," says Dave, slotting a Slayer CD into the machine. "I can't believe this. Is this really happening? I still am a fan. I'm more of a fan than I am a player in the band. I'm just like the kids I play for, I guess. I mean, I enjoy listening to the music. I get into it so much. The energy. The energy. There's no weak point.

It's just, the music, the way I feel it. When I play, I give it everything. I know every kid in that arena would love to be doing the exact same thing if they could. I'm just one of the lucky ones."

"I'll tell you honest," Eddie is saying as the burgers are served in a greasy spoon on the Sunset Strip. "One time when Kerry called me, my phone went flying off the bed. It really did. You know, the cord was sticking straight up and the phone was, like, swinging around the room, and I'm just, like, sitting there watching my phone go crazy. I was totally straight. I didn't even know what drugs were about at the time. Finally, I caught the phone and I pulled it down and like, 'Hello?' And it was Kerry. He was like, 'What the hell are you doing?'"

Eddie's real name is Laura. She's the assistant to a regional sales rep for a large national firm. She's also Slayer's biggest fan. It started years ago in Houston, when she was in ninth grade, living in the suburbs with her parents. Her father was the manager of a dry-cleaning plant. Her mother, a former big-band singer, had been reborn as a strict Baptist.

Laura was going through a kind of rebellious stage when she found heavy metal. She learned about it from a guy named Venom at a concert given by a Christian band called the Ethereals. Venom listened to Iron Maiden and Motörhead. And he listened to Venom. That was his favorite band. Venom wore leather and chains and safety pins. He was very cute.

Laura started calling herself Eddie. She dyed her hair jet black, wore leather, metal studs, skull rings. She liked her new music, but kept thinking, *There's got to be something heavier.* Then she heard Slayer's song "Chapel of Sin." There was this solo on it by Hanneman that made her feel like she was underwater and she couldn't catch her breath. She was just like, Oh, my God, this is incredible! And the words. She doesn't know why—*Harlots of hell/Spread your wings as I penetrate your soul,* you wouldn't think she'd dig something like that— but damn, it was good. It just went right through her, just made her go wooooooooow! It was like, she could listen to it, and then she was in a really good mood. Hearing "Chapel of Sin," that was it. She vowed right then and there, Slayer was her band.

See, weird things had always happened in her life. Like her mom would walk in and find her levitating near the ceiling. She'd call out *Laura!* and the girl would just drop down to the bed. And there were the visitors. They were hooded people, she doesn't know who. She called them the Council. The members of the Council never spoke, but they showed her things, pictures. To this day she'll see something, like a déjà vu, and remember that it was something they showed her. And one time, when she was seventeen or eighteen, she had troops marching through her house. Her dad was asleep on the couch. She was like, "Daddy, wake up, we got to get a priest in here." Daddy wouldn't wake up. She called her girlfriend. The friend asked, "What's all that rumbling in the background?"

Eddie joined the Doom Society, a kind of fan club that brought heavy metal bands to Houston. They got some press when they sacrificed a stack of Mötley Crüe albums to Slayer in an occult ceremony outside a radio station. It was a majorly outfreakish event, way cool. They drew a crowd. Eddie loved Slayer because they were fast, and there was just such power behind their music. It assaulted her. She could feel it. There was nothing like it. She got a buzz from it. She and her friends would have thrash sessions; they'd put on Slayer and pile on top of each other and just let it all out.

What were they letting out? She doesn't know exactly. Something about being a teenager. Something about living on this planet in these times. It's like, sometimes you want to scream, you know? It just feels great, great and free. They can put on an album and just slam into each other, just totally have fun in the privacy of their own rooms.

To Eddie's thinking, Slayer has become more and more popular because of what she calls "the slayerness of it all," the majorly fucked-up state of the world. At home, at school, on television, one thing is clear: Life sucks. Slayer commiserates. The demon on the stage recites truths that the kids in the audience already know inside themselves. Only when someone else says it do they know they aren't alone. And once that sinks in, and they see how hopeless everything is, the music and the buzz and the headbanging and all the rest helps them let it out, purge, a joyous, unified, tearless, savage good cry.

"It's like that song, 'Temptation,'" says Eddie, dipping a french fry in ketchup. "It gets to me because it says, 'Have you ever wondered why it's evil you're attracted to?' You know, I do wonder why. There's just so many people out there that are supposed to be on the good side, but they're not for real. Politicians, teachers, parents, ministers, Christians, everybody. They're hypocrites. The whole society. All the adults. They're so phony."

Eddie pauses a moment, lets her emotions run past. She looks over toward the door. In profile, the bright California sunlight makes her hazel eyes look yellow.

"I get frustrated," she says. "I try to keep things fine and wonderful, but, shit, talk about an angry sleeper. I wake up and my blanket is ripped to shreds, and oh, my God, my head will be inside a hole in the blanket, strangling me. I don't know how I do these things. In my sleep. Strangling myself. Just a majorly outfreakish event. Weird, huh?"

PERMISSIONS

"Temple of Doom" was assigned by *Rolling Stone* and published in GQ 6/94. A longer, Author's Cut version was later published in *Scary Monsters and Super Freaks* (Thunder's Mouth Press 2003). Reprinted with the permission of the author.

"The Death of a High School Narc" was first published in *Rolling Stone* 6/2/88. A longer, Author's Cut version was later published in *Scary Monsters and Super Freaks* (Thunder's Mouth Press 2003). Reprinted with the permission of the author.

"Raised in Captivity" is based on earlier work in *Rolling Stone* (two columns in Sager's regular column *Livin in the USA*, featuring art by Mary Ellen Mark). This story was published ten years later, in GQ 6/97, after Fannon was released from prison. A longer, Author's Cut version was later published in *Scary Monsters and Super Freaks* (Thunder's Mouth Press 2003). Reprinted with the permission of the author.

"Revenge of the Donut Boys" was published in *Rolling Stone* 10/01/92, in Sager's regular column *Livin in the USA*, featuring art by Mary Ellen Mark. A longer, Author's Cut version was later published in *Revenge of the Donut Boys* (Thunder's Mouth Press 2007). That book was reissued by The Sager Group LLC in 2018. Reprinted with the permission of the author.

"Death in Venice" was first published in *Rolling Stone* 9/22/1988. A longer, Author's Cut version was later published in *Wounded Warriors* (Da Capo Press, an imprint of Perseus Books Group, 2008.) It was later published with added details and information in *A Boy and His Dog in Hell* (The Sager Group LLC 2021). Reprinted with the permission of the author.

"Fact: Five out of Five Kids Who Kill Love Slayer" was first published in *Esquire* 02/92. A longer, Author's Cut version was later published in *Revenge of the Donut Boys* (Thunder's Mouth Press 2007). That book was reissued by The Sager Group LLC in 2018. Reprinted with the permission of the author.

ABOUT THE AUTHOR

Mike Sager is a best-selling author and award-winning reporter. A former *Washington Post* staff writer, contributing editor to *Rolling Stone*, and writer-at-large at *GQ*, he has written for *Esquire* for more than thirty years. Sager is the author or editor of more than a dozen books, including anthologies, novels, a biography, and textbooks. In 2010 he won the National Magazine Award for profile writing. A number of his stories have inspired films and documentaries; he is editor and publisher of The Sager Group LLC. For more information, please see MikeSager.com.

ABOUT THE PUBLISHERS

NeoText is a publisher of quality fiction and long-form journalism. Visit the NeoText website at NeoTextCorp.com.

The Sager Group was founded in 1984. In 2012 it was chartered as a multimedia content brand, with the intent of empowering those who create art—an umbrella beneath which makers can pursue, and profit from, their craft directly, without gatekeepers. TSG publishes books; ministers to artists and provides modest grants; and produces documentary, feature, and commercial films. By harnessing the means of production, The Sager Group helps artists help themselves. For more information, please see TheSagerGroup.net.

Artifex Te Adiuva